Pathways to Armageddon
...AND BEYOND

BETTY LYNN

HARVEST HOUSE PUBLISHERS
EUGENE, OREGON 97402

PATHWAYS TO ARMAGEDDON

Copyright © 1992 by Harvest House Publishers
Eugene, Oregon 97402

Library of Congress Cataloging-in-Publication Data

Lynn, Betty, 1951– .
    Pathways to Armageddon / Betty Lynn.
    ISBN 0-89081-930-0
    1. Bible—Prophecies—Armageddon.   2. Armageddon—
    Biblical teaching.   3. World politics—1945— .   I. Title.
    BS649.A68L96   1992   91-38066
    220.1'5—dc20   CIP

Printed in the United States of America.

About the Author

A committed Christian who has been fascinated by Bible prophecy since childhood, Betty Lynn has actively studied the prophetic Word for more than 20 years. This rich background combined with her diverse interests in such areas as international politics, history, religion, and science have uniquely qualified her as an astute observer of our times.

Ms. Lynn is the Research Editor for the Omega Letter Publishing Group of Niagara Falls, New York. In addition to providing the group with an analysis of current events, she has been a frequent contributor to the *Omega Letter* and *Christian World Report*. While avidly pursuing her prophetic avocations, Betty is also employed as a manager for a major broadcasting company.

To my parents,
who grounded me in the Word
and introduced me to my beloved Lord,

and

To my best friends,
Larry and Ann,
without whose loving encouragement
and advice this book
could not have been written.

FOREWORD

When we founded The Omega-Letter Publishing Group almost eight years ago we wondered if there would be enough material to fill a monthly newsletter with current fulfillments of Bible prophecy. Now in the early 90's, three full-sized publications, regular video reports, and a weekly television program can barely keep up with it all.

The reason is simple. Jesus told us that the signs of his coming would be like birth pangs—becoming ever closer together and more intense. Today this is exactly what is happening. The foundations of the world as we know it are being changed forever. A fundamental shift is underway.

However, there is much more to it than that. With the world's attention riveted on the European Community, the tiny state of Israel, the Middle East, and the Commonwealth of Independent States, it is becoming clear to longtime students of Bible prophecy that what we are witnessing is a specific pattern, a pattern of occurrences that the Bible said would precede the second coming of Christ!

With the explosion of events in our age we have desperately needed a book that would dig below the surface and provide an indepth look at the roots and future outcomes of today's headlines. Betty Lynn's book does just that. It is a thought-provoker that will spark exciting debates. For the prophecy enthusiast who wants something deeper than the standard prophecy books which proliferate today, *Pathways to Armageddon* is well worth the read!

—Peter Lalonde

INTRODUCTION

One could fill a library just with recent books on prophetic subjects. Many of these books are primers for the layman which cover the entire gamut of prophetic topics. Any number of them could be recommended to the lay reader.

This book assumes that the reader is somewhat familiar with the prophetic Word and has read at least one foundational book on the topic. While an effort has been made to avoid overwhelming the lay reader, much of the basic material found in these other works has been assumed.

It is the intent of this book to provide the believing Christian with an analysis of historical and current-event trends in the light of biblical prophecy that suggest that his Lord, Jesus Christ, is about to appear.

CONTENTS

1

Pathways to
the Future

━━━━━━━━━━━━━━ ✦ ━━━━━━━━━━━━━━

Who doesn't long for the good old days, when life in the world was like an old familiar pathway? Our steps were familiar, for we knew the exact position of each societal stone and root. Our confidence lay in the path's predictability and our knowledge of its twists and turns. But now those days seem gone forever!

The world has become truly unpredictable:

- Death lurks at our doorsteps as violent crime touches every nation and neighborhood.
- Fear and uncertainty dominate our society.
- Basic institutions and power structures, such as the nation-state and financial systems, are being undermined on a world scale.

Our mental and emotional terra firma can be seismically shaken each time we read our newspapers. Only those with hearts of stone are untouched by the victims of senseless violence, oppression, and natural catastrophe. The news can not only leave us despairing but bewildered. Have you noticed that nothing in the final

analysis is what it initially appeared to be? Talk of
global peace is immediately followed by acts of war. The
"triumph of democracy" is celebrated by a new age of
dictatorship.

There is no shortage of people willing to explain modern life to us. Who can escape the predictions of these
modern-day prophets on the nightly news? The Middle
East analysts, the Kremlinologists, the economists, and
the psychologists all bombard us with their understanding of our present and their visions of our future.
But as time passes, we find that our media prognostica-
tors are rarely right.

The world asks, "Is the pathway to the future so dark
and unknowable? Is there nothing we can know for
sure?" We in the Judeo-Christian community know the
answer, and there is good news: There is a sovereign
God who is the Lord of Hosts, the God of Israel. He is
the Creator of the heavens and the earth, and having
formed His creation, He has not abandoned us.

Through the gift of His Word, the Bible, the future is
not dark and unknowable; God has revealed a future
about which we can be certain. Through His Word, God
provides us with wisdom for today. This "owner's man-
ual" for the human spirit gives us the information we
need to live wholesome and righteous lives. His Word
also provides us with an outline of future events. It
describes human history, with some events leading to
judgment and others leading to a restoration of the
habitation of God with men. Armed with this information, we can prepare for those future circumstances.
Either through wisdom for today or hope for tomorrow,
the Word of God changes our lives!

Prophecy and the Nature of God

God's prophecies of the future address not only the

actions of human beings, but also those special times when God intervenes in human affairs. Therefore, in addition to causing us to reevaluate and redirect our own lives, prophecy also gives us deeper insight into the nature of the God whom we serve.

God's Existence and Presence

When God intervenes in human affairs, He proves that He is living and active. Each time God dramatically accomplishes what He promised, He is affirming His own existence. Even the act of providing us with the verifiable prophetic Word is proof of His existence. As Daniel told King Nebuchadnezzar when beginning to interpret his divinely inspired dream:

> As for the mystery about which the king has inquired, neither wise men, conjurers, magicians, nor diviners are able to declare it to the king. However, there is a God in heaven who reveals mysteries, and He has made known to King Nebuchadnezzar what will take place in the latter days (Daniel 2:27,28).

Prophecy graphically demonstrates God's *omnipresence*—His ability to be everywhere concurrently. He transcends time and space even though we are bound by it. The past, present, and future are one unified event to Him. It is God's omnipresence that facilitates His ability to reveal the future with 100 percent accuracy.

For those of us living in the here-and-now, this is a difficult concept to get our mental arms around. It is this difficulty in stretching our thinking beyond our own circumstances which causes some people to believe that because God foretells the future, He also fully prescribes and orders it. This is not true, for *full* control would compromise man's free will. God frequently intervenes in the affairs of this world, but He has not fully scripted our future. He sees the choices we will make in response to His workings, but He does not make our choices for us.

God's Knowledge

Prophecy also demonstrates the *omniscience* of God— His ability to know all things. Our knowledge is limited to our personal experience of the past and present, but His knowledge is full and complete.

God has a full knowledge of not only the past and present, but also of the future—not just the future of actualities, but also the future of possibilities. Many prophecies are unconditional, and these foretold events will become actualities. However, many other prophecies are *conditional*—that is, "if you do not change 'this,' then 'that' will happen." These reflect God's knowledge of future possibility.

By sharing His knowledge of the future of possibility, God gives us the opportunity to modify our behavior and thereby the future of actuality. An example of this type of prophecy was the one uttered by Jonah against Nineveh. The people of the city took advantage of the warning, repented of their sin, and were spared a future filled with the judgment of God.

The fulfillment of prophecy confirms God's knowledge and proves that He is a reliable witness of all human events, whether past, present, or future.

God's Sovereignty

Prophecy also affirms the *sovereignty* of God—His ability and right to reign over all creation. By His creative right and power, He has dominion over all things. It is at His pleasure that kings rule; He is truly the King of Kings.

Sometimes when God exercises His sovereign right and employs willing people to accomplish His purposes, they mistakenly believe they have achieved their ends by their own might. When Israel sinned, God used the Assyrians to punish them. When the King of Assyria became haughty, thinking that he had conquered Israel by his own might, God asked rhetorically:

> Is the axe to boast itself over the one who chops with it? Is the saw to exalt itself over the one who wields it? That would be like a club wielding those who lift it, or like a rod lifting him who is not wood (Isaiah 10:15).

In the book of Revelation we are shown a future scene in heaven when God is enthroned in His heaven and all creation attests to His sovereignty and dominion:

> Every created thing which is in heaven and on the earth and under the earth and on the sea, and all things in them, I heard saying, "To Him who sits on the throne, and to the Lamb, be blessing and honor and glory and dominion forever and ever" (Revelation 5:13).

It is because of God's sovereignty that we can rest in the assurance that nothing will ever happen in His universe which will thwart or abrogate His promises to us.

God's Justice

Prophecy proclaims *God's right and intention to judge mankind*. God has created people and set before them a standard of conduct. All will stand before Him and have their deeds judged. There are those who believe that a loving God could never sit in judgment and condemn people, but they must remember that when His only Son, the Messiah, took upon himself the sins of others, God did not shrink from judging Him.

Prophecy shows us that God, who did not spare His own Son, will be no less severe in His judgment of defiant men. For those who live in opposition to God and His people, this is terrifying news, for there will be no escape. For those whose sins have been forgiven and who worship Him, this is welcome news, for they can know that their oppression by evildoers will be avenged.

God's Faithfulness

Biblical prophecy overflows with the manifold promises of God to His people. All of these would be meaningless if God were not faithful. But He *is* faithful to perform every word of His promises despite the failing of mankind. It is through the faithfulness of God that the people of Israel have been preserved, despite the contrary efforts of mankind and Satan.

When God's Son returns in glory to fight at the battle called Armageddon, he too will be identified by his faithfulness:

> I saw heaven opened; and behold, a white horse, and He who sat upon it is called Faithful and True; and in righteousness He judges and wages war (Revelation 19:11).

The fulfillment of the prophetic Word demonstrates God's faithfulness in living up to His Word. All that He has spoken will be done. He is totally trustworthy.

Prophecy and Faith

While many people undervalue prophecy, this Almighty God who reveals Himself through it considers prophecy very important. God has indicated the importance of prophecy by its sheer volume in His Word: More than a quarter of the entire Bible is prophetic!

Jesus also believed that prophecy was important. When He met two of His disciples on the road to Emmaus after His resurrection, He scolded them for their ignorance of the prophetic Word:

> He said to them, "O foolish men and slow of heart to believe in all that the prophets have spoken! Was it not necessary for the Christ to suffer these things and to enter into His glory?" And beginning with Moses and with all the prophets, He explained to them the things concerning Himself in all the Scriptures (Luke 24:25-27).

Jesus frequently counseled His disciples to "Watch!" for the fulfillments of biblical prophecy—the signs of His return. If God has placed such importance on sharing His knowledge of the future with us, then it is equally important for us to work hard at understanding His Word. The study of prophecy has a high "sweat quotient," but the rewards are great, much like mining rich ores: You must search through a lot of rock to find and collect nuggets, then refine and mold them.

Pathways to the Future

Human events are a sequential continuum. Historical circumstances have delivered us to where we are today, and the things which transpire today will shape our future. Although our God is still in the miracle business, most prophetic events will be fulfilled by the natural outworking of trends in human behavior and the forces of nature. These events will not materialize out of thin air. That sort of mystical approach to prophecy builds a wall between the Word and believability. Discussing prophecies without addressing their historical context is irresponsible and sometimes leads to great misunderstandings. It is like trying to understand a two-hour movie with many twisted subplots based on a five-minute clip.

In this book we will be looking at historical developments and trends in our day which may lead to the fulfillment of biblical prophecy. We will limit our discussions to geopolitical trends or "pathways." This historical perspective will greatly assist our understanding of the future. Connecting prophecy to our past and present will also help us integrate our knowledge of future events into our sense of reality.

God's biblical prophets have described major and minor happenings on numerous pathways. For example, they frequently addressed the pathway of spiritual and social development. Other sections of this pathway are marked apostasy, New Age movement, ecumenism, societal decay, and spiritual deception. The pathway of nature was also widely addressed. This pathway is an increasingly dark one, characterized by a diminished ozone layer, earthquakes, pollution, plagues, and pestilence. These pathways are treated well by many other authors and will not be addressed further here.

This book focuses on six geopolitical pathways. We will examine the full course of these pathways and attempt to integrate the steps from our current position to key future events described by God's prophets. Some of the things we will discuss are speculative, and are presented to show how easily today's current events can lead to the fulfillment of prophecy and the establishment of God's kingdom on earth.

The six geopolitical pathways which we will examine are:

The Pathway of Government

We will discuss the development and dissolution of the nation-state system and how it will be replaced by a system of world government. Will this trend in government lead to the creation of the final world order predicted by God's prophets?

The Pathway of Power

Here we will look at the triumph and defeat of universal democracy in our day, and the rising trend toward monarchy. Will this movement leave the door ajar for the Antichrist to enter and slip onto his universal throne?

The European Pathway

While the rest of the world has been critically weakened by colossal debt, Europe has been taking "economic steroids." At the end of the twentieth century, economic muscle is the truest form of power. Is Europe about to conquer the world, not by force, but by financial seduction?

The Russian Pathway

The Soviet Union has become a historical postscript. But before its epitaph is written, does it have one vicious, military move up its sleeve?

The Arab/Moslem Pathway

During the Gulf War, some in the religious community condemned coalition action against Iraq. Was the Gulf War the beginning of the biblically predicted judgment of Babylon and a personal act of God? What is the destiny of the Arab/Moslem nations?

The Israeli Pathway

God is becoming increasingly active in the affairs of Israel. How is Israel being prepared to host the messianic kingdom?

One common feature of all these pathways is that they are all headed downhill. Jesus used the simile of "birth pangs" to describe the growing speed and intensity of end time events. Indeed, that is what we are experiencing today.

Along each of these pathways lie major milestone events. These milestones are major prophetic events which in most cases have been extensively described by God's prophets. These events are the key turning points on our pathways. Our understanding of these prophetic milestones is essential to our understanding of current trends, for it is by these milestones that we see the ever-closer return of our Lord. These are the guideposts to our blessed hope.

2

PROPHETIC
MILESTONES

When walking along a pathway through a forest, it is easy to get lost unless you are familiar with features of the terrain. The same is true of the prophetic pathways: We need theological reference points. In a forest, we might take note of a particular rock or tree and establish it as a place marker or "milestone." To help us find our way on our geopolitical pathways, we will become proficient in identifying several key prophetic milestones.

We need to become so familiar with the features of these milestones that we would recognize them in the dark. Because we will be discussing only the geopolitical *pathways*, we will limit our discussion to major geopolitical *milestones* as well. Many of the world's pathways intersect at these milestone events.

As we walk along each pathway, we will find that each time we pass an intersection, we will encounter one of these major events. One common feature of these milestones is that they all lie along the Israeli pathway. This is because Israel is the key to God's plan for the ages. Israel is the bearer of all God's promises, and for this she has been viciously pursued by God's enemies. For if she could be destroyed, God could be proven a liar. But our

Major Geopolitical Milestones

Geopolitical Milestone	Principal Prophetic Reference	Intersecting Pathways
Middle East Peace Covenant	Daniel 9:24-27	Europe, Israel, many others
Russo-Israeli War	Ezekiel 38,39	Russia, Arab/Moslem, Israel
Kingdom of the Evil Prince	Daniel 2,7	Worldwide Europe, Israel
Armageddon and the Advent of Messiah	Zechariah 12,14	Worldwide Europe, Israel
Messianic Kingdom	Revelation 20	Worldwide Israel
Eternal Kingdom	Revelation 20-22	Worldwide Israel

Milestones on the Israeli Pathway

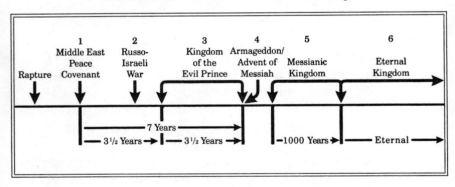

omnipotent God stands guard over Israel. In the near future, many more attempts will be made to destroy this tiny nation. In fact, a couple of the milestones that we will be examining have the destruction of Israel as their primary motive—but they will not succeed. The Guardian of Israel never slumbers nor sleeps, but is ever watchful!

Middle East Peace Covenant

The pathways of Europe and Israel will soon intersect at the milestone of the Middle East Peace Covenant. This treaty may be very broad and involve many other nations, but at a bare minimum Europe will legally become the guarantor of Israel's peace. The principal architect of this treaty will be "the prince"—a man commonly referred to as the Antichrist.[1]

This covenant and its architect appears in a prophecy of Daniel.[2] The prophet Daniel described a period of time that stretches from the restoration of Jerusalem after Israel's Babylonian captivity until the establishment of the messianic kingdom. He tells us that God's timepiece for these events was set to 490 years. That divine stopwatch would—

- ♦ begin when Israel was given a decree allowing them to rebuild Jerusalem;

- ♦ stop after 483 years (69 "sevens" or weeks of years), when Messiah the Prince would be killed or "cut off" and Jerusalem would again be destroyed, this time by the people of the coming prince; and

- ♦ restart when that evil prince makes a covenant with "the many."

Historically, we know that the seventy "weeks" of years began to tick away when King Artaxerxes of Persia issued a decree allowing Nehemiah and his fellow Israelis to return to their land and rebuild the walls of Jerusalem in 445 B.C.[3]

Exactly 483 years later,[4] a young itinerant preacher named Yeshua (Jesus) who had made messianic claims was condemned by the Israeli courts and executed by the Roman government. The watch stopped. In keeping with Daniel's prophecy, His death was followed approximately 40 years later by the destruction of Jerusalem and the temple by the armies of Europe led by the city-state of Rome.

We are now waiting for the stopwatch to resume and tick off the remaining seven years. What wisdom does Daniel share with us about that time?

During the final seven years of Daniel's vision a prominent, satanically empowered leader will arise. This "prince who is to come" will be European. We know this because Daniel tells us that the prince is from the people who destroyed "the city and the sanctuary." That dubious honor was claimed by the armies of Europe led by Rome. That prince will author a seven-year treaty with "the many." Some people believe that "the many" refers strictly to the people of Israel. However, it is possible that it may mean "many nations." If this interpretation is accurate, it would be in keeping with the frantic international search for a comprehensive Middle East peace agreement.

Daniel does not describe the details of the covenant. However, we do know that Satan is a great imitator. He frequently offers mankind a cheap substitute that closely resembles God's original promise. Given this understanding of the enemy, perhaps we can reasonably anticipate the terms of the coming Middle East Peace Covenant.

In Ezekiel 37:26-28 we find another covenant. This one contains the original promises of God:

> I will make a covenant of peace with them; it will be an everlasting covenant with them. And I will place them and multiply them, and I will set My sanctuary in their midst forever. My dwelling place also will be with them; and I will be their God, and they will be My people. And the nations will know that I am the Lord who sanctifies Israel, when My sanctuary is in their midst forever.

If we assume that this is the model for the prince's counterfeit covenant, and given our current understanding of world affairs, we can anticipate what the terms of this agreement might be.

Details of the Counterfeit Covenant

First, we can expect it to be a *peace* covenant. The term of the peace covenant which God will enter into is "everlasting." The cut-rate version can be expected to have an original term of seven years, and as we know, the prince will break the terms after only 3½ years. Current events would suggest that this covenant will generally guarantee the security of Israel in exchange for territory and other concessions. One might question whether it is a "peace" covenant or a "piece" covenant!

Article I:

God's covenant states "I will *place* them," which refers to even more ancient covenants in which God has deeded to Israel the territory from the Nile River to the Euphrates River (Ezekiel 37:25; Genesis 35:12; 15:18-21). We can expect the imitation covenant to be less generous. Conventional wisdom would indicate that Israel will probably be offered and accept less territory than it now occupies. Territorial concessions will probably be made, at least in the Gaza strip, and perhaps even on the West Bank, if guarantees regarding Israel's water supply are assured.

Article II:

God's covenant states "I will... *multiply* them." One of the ways we are told that God will multiply them is by regathering the sons and daughters of Israel from among the nations (Ezekiel 37:21). Perhaps the prince's version will provide modest guarantees of immigration rights. In light of current events, this might mean providing direct flights from the former Soviet Union and other countries to Israel. Or perhaps, it might involve opening the capitals of Europe to act as gateways for all Eastern European immigration to Israel. It may also include provisions that the Arabs drop their campaign to stop Israeli immigration at all cost.

Article III:

God promises "I will set *My sanctuary* in their midst forever." This would indicate that the third temple will be built on Temple Mount in Jerusalem. Although Israel has had sovereignty over Jerusalem from 1967, the Temple Mount is still under the control of the Waqf, the Muslim Supreme Religious Council. We can expect that using pseudo-Solomonic wisdom, as part of the prince's covenant, the territory and administration of Temple Mount will be divided between the Arabs and the Israelis. This will give the Jews the legal grounds they require to begin temple service.

There is additional scriptural support for this conjecture. In Revelation 11:1,2 we read: "There was given me a measuring rod like a staff; and someone said, 'Rise and measure the temple of God, and the altar, and those who worship in it. And leave out the court which is outside the temple, and do not measure it, for it has been given to the nations; and they will tread under foot the holy city for forty-two months.'" The court just south of the ancient location of the temple currently contains the Dome of the Rock and the El Aqsa Mosque. Perhaps they will remain. The prince's involvement with the reinstituting of temple service will further certify his false messianic credentials.

Finally, God promises that *"My dwelling place* will be with them, and I will be their God." This would suggest that the Shekinah glory—the Presence of God—will return to the holy of holies and Israel will worship their God in spirit and in truth. Although not a term of the agreement, we will see this presence and role imitated as well. In 2 Thessalonians 2:4 we read that the prince— the man of lawlessness, the son of destruction—"takes his seat in the temple of God, displaying himself as being God." He not only imitates the divine presence, but he also attempts to assume the role as Israel's God.

Whatever the terms, when the prince enters into this treaty with Israel, the divine stopwatch will begin its final countdown.

The Rapture

Before that countdown starts, I believe there will be another event of great personal importance to each of us. That event is popularly called the "rapture." This rapture or catching away has strong parallels in ancient Jewish wedding customs. The Bible often uses the simile of a bridegroom and bride to describe the relationship between Messiah and the body of those who faithfully follow Him.[5]

Zola Levitt has produced a wonderful booklet called *A Christian Love Story* which addresses this simile in detail. In it he says:

When the young man of Israel in Jesus' time saw
the girl he wanted (or the girl his father said he
wanted), he would approach her with a marriage
contract.... The bridegroom would present himself
to the bride with this agreement, offering to pay a
suitable price for her, and she and her father would
consider his contract. If the terms were suitable,
the bride and groom would drink a cup of wine
together and this would seal the bargain. This cup
was most significant. It signified the bridegroom's
willingness to sacrifice in order to have this bride.
It was offered as a toast to the bride, and of course it
showed the bride's willingness to enter into this
marriage. Then the groom would pay the price. It
should be said that this price was no modest token
but was set so that the new bride would be a costly
item—that was the idea.... When that matter was
settled the groom would depart. He would make a
little speech to his bride, saying, "I go to prepare a
place for you," and he would return to his father's
house. Back at his father's house, he would build
her a bridal chamber, a little mansion, in which
they would have their future honeymoon.... The
bride, for her part, was obliged to do a lot of waiting.... Finally the chamber would be ready and
the bridegroom would assemble his young friends
to accompany him on the exciting trip to claim his
bride. The big moment had arrived and the bridegroom was more than ready, we can be sure. He and
his young men would set out in the night, making
every attempt to completely surprise the bride.
And that's the romantic part—all the Jewish brides
were "stolen."... Actually, as the excited party of
young men would get close to her house, they were
obliged to give her a warning. Someone in the wedding party would shout. When the bride heard that
shout, she knew her young man would be there

momentarily. She had only time to light her lamp, grab her honeymoon clothing and go. Her sisters and bridesmaids who wanted to attend also had to have their lamps trimmed and ready, of course.... And so the groom and his men would charge in, grab the girls and make off with them!... When the wedding party reached the house of the groom's father, the bride and groom would go into their chamber and shut the door. No one else would enter.[6]

An examination of the Gospels shows us rich parallels between these wedding customs and Jesus' words and deeds. For example, when Jesus offered His disciples the cup at the Passover feast, just before His death, He was symbolically proposing marriage to all of His followers. By their partaking of that same cup, they entered into contract with Him—they became His bride. If you partake of the Lord's Supper, think about this rich symbolism in your next worship service.

Jesus' bride, because she had broken God's law, was under the divine penalty of death. The agreed-upon bride price was Jesus substitutionary death. He gave his life that His beloved might live.

After He paid His bride's debt, He arose and went to His Father's house to begin construction of their dwelling place. Prior to His death, He sought to console His bride by reminding her of His return:

Let not your heart be troubled; believe in God, believe also in Me. In My Father's house are many dwelling places; if it were not so, I would have told you; for I go to prepare a place for you. And if I go and prepare a place for you, I will come again, and receive you to Myself; that where I am, there you may be also (John 14:1-3).

Awaiting the Bridegroom

There is great theological dispute whether Messiah will return to catch away His bride before, during, or after the term of the coming Peace Covenant. Although I am not dogmatic about it, I personally believe that He will come for His bride *before* the Covenant is signed, for these reasons:

- ◆ The seven-year term of the Covenant will be coincident with divine judgments being poured out upon the earth. Much of the book of Revelation describes these judgments.

  If the Bridegroom's family is about to devastate the bride's hometown, does it not make sense that they would get her out of there first?

  If the intent of those judgments is to punish the rebellious, would the Bridegroom choose to allow His faithful bride to suffer the same end He has reserved for His enemies?

- ◆ The similes which Jesus used to describe that seven-year period of judgment compared those times to the days of Noah[7] and Lot.[8] In the case of Noah, the faithful were sealed away in an ark while the rest of the world was judged and destroyed. In the case of Lot, divine messengers were sent to remove Lot and his loved ones from "ground zero" immediately prior to the blast. Given these two dramatic rescues as comparisons, does it make sense that God would allow His faithful ones to remain on earth during an unprecedented period of distress and judgment?

I don't think so! I think that Messiah's love, concern, and desire for His bride are too great. I believe that prior to the signing of the Covenant, and prior to divine judgment, Messiah will catch His bride away.

Are you Messiah's bride? Do you expect to be taken with Him when He comes? We have all been judged guilty by God for breaking His law. We have all been sentenced to eternal death. Have you sought out Messiah? Have you entered into contract with Him and allowed Him to pay a bride price for you? He died for you! Just as the men of Israel would approach God's temple and present a substitutionary sacrifice, have you presented God with Messiah's substitutionary death to void your own penalty?

Beloved one, there is no greater love than this. Jesus has already paid the price, and all you have to do is enter into contract with Him and authorize payment. And once you have, you will be part of that messianic bride. You will be part of that great company of believers who faithfully watch for His coming to catch them away. You will be spared the horrific judgments that are about to be meted out upon this rebellious world.

If you haven't already, why don't you take a few moments to enter into contract with Messiah Jesus right now?

If you are part of that messianic bride, are you expectantly awaiting the arrival of your Bridegroom? Although it may seem hard to believe, soon you will be looking deeply into the eyes of your Beloved.

At the rapture, Messiah will physically transform us; alive or dead, we will be resurrected. In an instant your aging, achy, disease-prone body will be overhauled and given an eternal warranty. Your new body will be immortal.[9] Then we will each appear before His "judgment seat." Unfortunately, this is where many Christians get

panicky. However, this "judgment" is better likened to
the judgment of a sporting event rather than the judgment of a criminal case. Our success in leading a faithful
life will be evaluated. Our Bridegroom will reward each
act of faithfulness to Him and His purposes.[10] He will
purge away our selfish and sinful acts.[11] The preparation for the wedding will then be complete. For seven
years we will attend a "reception" in our new home, the
"New Jerusalem"!

While this world is witnessing the signing of the
Middle East Peace Covenant and enduring the less-
than-tender ministrations of the "prince who is to
come," you and I will be off honeymooning with Messiah!

The Russo-Israeli War

A massive invasion of Israel has been described by the
prophet Ezekiel. The Russian, Arab/Moslem, and Israeli pathways will violently collide at a milestone
called the Russo-Israeli War. In chapters 38 and 39,
Ezekiel describes a lightning-fast attack on the small
Jewish state. These chapters describe the planning,
execution, and outcome of a war mounted by Russia
and her radical Moslem allies. Were it not for God's
intervention, this would be the point at which modern
Israel would cease to exist.

Before we discuss the nature of this invasion in
detail, let's look at how it fits into the overall prophetic timeline. First of all, Scripture is unclear as to
the exact timing of this event relative to other prophetic events. Although it is hard to say definitively,
I believe that this invasion will occur during the
first half of the seven-year Covenant. My reasons are
these:

- *It will be preceded by massive immigration to Israel.*

  Ezekiel 37 describes the rebirth of the nation of Israel. The very next chapters describe this invasion. Ezekiel tells us that this invasion occurs in "the latter years," after Israel is regathered from the nations of her dispersion:

  > After many days you will be summoned; *in the latter years* you will come into the land that is restored from the sword, whose inhabitants have been gathered from many nations to the mountains of Israel which had been a continual waste; but its people were brought out from the nations, and they are living securely, all of them (Ezekiel 38:8).

  That "ingathering," specifically from Russia, is occurring in our day. Therefore I expect that the invasion will occur sooner rather than later. In fact it could occur at any time.

- *It should occur after the rapture.*

  The Bible indicates that the return of Messiah for His bride, in keeping with Jewish marital custom, will be a surprise.[12] When this event takes place, it will send off theological skyrockets. If the invasion of Israel were to occur before the rapture, it seems that the element of surprise would be compromised. Therefore it is probable that the invasion will come after the rapture and signing of the Covenant.

- *It will occur when Israel is at peace, and therefore after the Middle East Peace Covenant and before the reign of the evil prince.*

At the time of the invasion, Ezekiel describes Israel as dwelling in peace (38:8,11). I do not believe that this will be true prior to the Covenant, in that guaranteeing Israel's peace will be its primary purpose. Nor do I believe that Israel could be considered at peace during the second half of the seven years, for the prince will be very busy oppressing and attempting to annihilate Israel.

- *The Russo-Israeli war could be the "second seal" in Revelation.*

The book of Revelation describes judgments which will occur on the earth throughout the seven years of the Covenant. The first set of judgments which are described are released by the breaking of seals within a scroll. It is generally regarded that these judgments occur in the first half of the seven years. As each seal is broken, the scroll is unwound and the judgments are revealed. The first judgment is the entry of a conqueror who is given a crown. The second judgment is the replacement of peace with warfare:

> When He broke the second seal, I heard the second living creature saying, "Come." And another, a red horse, went out; and to him who sat on it, it was granted to take peace from the earth, and that men should

slay one another; and a great sword was given to him (Revelation 6:3,4).

It is important to notice that this war comes after a time of peace, much like the Russian invasion described by Ezekiel. Also, there is some similarity to the description of the fighting:

"I shall call for a sword against him on all My mountains," declares the Lord God. "Every man's sword will be against his brother" (Ezekiel 38:21).

This similarity between the second seal and the Russo-Israeli War may help to place the invasion in the first half of the Covenant's term.

Who are the participants in this invasion?

Son of man, set your face toward Gog of the land of Magog, the prince of Rosh, Meshech, and Tubal, and prophesy against him.... Persia, Ethiopia [Cush], and Put with them, all of them with shield and helmet; Gomer with all its troops; Beth-togarmah from the remote parts of the north with all its troops—many peoples with you (Ezekiel 38:2,5,6).

The prophet Ezekiel did not have a Rand McNally 1990's atlas available to him, so he could not use the modern place names with which we are familiar. Rather, he identified the invaders by their ancient tribal names. Our challenge is to correspond those tribal names to modern nations. Hammond's *Atlas of the Bible Lands* contains a map entitled "The Nations According to Genesis 10." This map shows the early settlements of these tribes. By comparing their placement on that map with a modern map of nations, we arrive at the following cross-reference (see next page).

Ezekiel identifies the leader of this invasion as "Gog, of the land of Magog, the prince of Rosh, Meshech and Tubal." Gog has been widely interpreted to be the head of the Soviet Union. Yet Gog is not described as "the King of the North," a singular leader of a unified people or nation. Rather, he is portrayed as a multitribal ringleader. He is a man who gathers together an army of like-minded peoples from tribes who are specifically named. By providing this detailed list of invaders which included several former Soviet tribes (see chart), perhaps Ezekiel has hinted at the breakup of the Soviet central government.

Gog is also described as the prince of "Rosh." Hal Lindsey explains the derivation of "Rosh":

The word literally means in Hebrew the "top" or "head" of something. According to most scholars, this word is used in the sense of a proper name, not as a descriptive noun qualifying the word "prince." The German scholar Dr. Keil says after a careful grammatical analysis that it should be translated as a proper name, i.e., Rosh. He says, "The Byzantine and Arabic writers frequently mention a people called Ros and Rus, dwelling in the country of Taurus, and reckoned among the Scythian tribes." Dr. Gesenius in his Hebrew Lexicon says, "... Rosh was a designation for the tribes then north of the Taurus Mountains, dwelling in the neighborhood of the Volga." He concluded that in this name and tribe we have the first historical trace of the Russ or Russian nation.[14]

Cross-Reference of
Tribal Locations and Modern Nations

Ezekiel 38:2-6	Early Tribal Locations[13]	Modern Nation
Rosh	Not shown	Russia
Magog	North of the Caspian Sea	Kazakhstan
Meshech	East of the Black Sea	Georgia and Northeast Turkey
Tubal	Southeast of the Black Sea	Northern Turkey
Persia	North of the Persian Gulf	Iran
Cush	Southern Nile valley	Ethiopia, Sudan
Put	West of Egypt	Libya
Gomer	North and south of the Black Sea	Ukraine, Southern Russia, Central Turkey
Togarmah	Southeast of the Black Sea	Eastern Turkey

Another of the invaders is "Gomer." Many fine expositors interpret Gomer to be modern Germany. This is in keeping with Jewish tradition. Until the late 1980's it was very easy to stand by this interpretation. East Germany was the largest Russian satellite in Eastern Europe. This was seen as a prophetic fulfillment of the relationship between "Rosh" and "Gomer." But when East Germany broke away from the Soviet Union and was reunited with West Germany, many interpreters were left speechless.

Perhaps Germany is not the tribe of Gomer mentioned in Ezekiel. On our cross-reference table, you can see that at least some maps indicate that "Gomer" originally settled in what is today the Ukraine, southern Russia, and Turkey before migrating westward. Therefore "Gomer" may not be Germany at all, but the Ukraine and her immediate neighbors. It should be noted that this area is heavily Moslem. Therefore these tribes would be religiously predisposed to joining a "holy war" against Israel.

We have established that the invasion will be led by Russia and will involve the Moslem southern republics. Also joining in the fray will be a number of Russian allies—her radical Moslem clients, including Iran, Libya, the Sudan, and Ethiopia. In addition, the maps would indicate that parts of modern Turkey may also be involved. Today that may seem a little farfetched, because Turkey is a member of NATO, and was part of the coalition against Iraq. However, President Ozal's involvement in the coalition was not popularly supported in Turkey, and contributed to his loss of power. We may yet see the Turkish government move into the radical Moslem camp.

What is the motive for this war? Ezekiel tells us that this invasion is inspired by two sources. First, Russian masterminds are developing yet another "evil plan"

(Ezekiel 38:10) all on their own. Second, God is hardening the invaders' hearts for judgment. Russia and her allies have been mistreating and persecuting God's people for centuries. For 70 years, Russia refused to even confess the existence of God. Ezekiel tells us that God Himself is "setting a hook" in Russia's jaw (38:4) to draw her down to her judgment.

In the light of current events, can we imagine how this "evil plan" will come about? It becomes easier with each passing day. We have already seen one hard-line "evil plan" which went awry. Now that the central government of the Soviet Union has disintegrated, and as broken but unbeaten hard-liners concoct new and improved plans to glue the nation back together, risky military adventures become more and more probable. Consider this Communist hard-liner logic:

> The democrats have destroyed the Soviet Union. It all began when we turned our backs on our friends and allied with our enemies.

> Our relationship with our Moslem friends was critically damaged by the Gulf War. Those misguided reformers, Gorbachev and Shevardnadze, not only denied our friends' support during the Gulf War, but they unleashed Western imperialism in the Middle East, and they have also allowed thousands upon thousands of Jews to immigrate to "Palestine."

> At home, our people are starving, angry, and are on the verge of revolution. The Jews have taken our precious resources, both their brains and our goods, (This must be so, for there are no consumer goods, and they were the only ones to leave!) Our Arab friends are angry that we have released the Jews, for they are now settling on Arab soil in Palestine.

We have a plan—an opportunity to kill two birds with one stone. Through it we can rekindle our friendship with our radical Moslem friends and at the same time restore our nation and its wealth. It's very simple: we invade Israel. It will take care of the Jewish immigration problem, it will throw the West into a state of confusion, we'll bring back our goods, and it will be popular with our citizenry. It will be a cakewalk, and we'll all be heroes!

Pharaoh himself couldn't have said it better! Some 3500 years ago the king of Egypt decided to let God's people go, only to go after them to retrieve them. It is interesting that the mass immigration of Soviet Jewry has been called "Operation Exodus." Just as Pharaoh lost his army pursuing the people of the original Exodus, so Russia will lose her army pursuing Soviet Jewry. Ezekiel 38:21 describes some of the early fighting as brother against brother. This may allude to Jewish Soviet immigrants fighting against their Russian brothers in uniform. Yet the defender of Israel will not be the Israeli Defense Force, but this time it will be God Himself. The God of Israel will miraculously and utterly destroy the invaders!

We are told in Ezekiel 39:12 that it will take Israel seven months to find and bury the dead invaders in order to cleanse the land. Perhaps this seven-month period gives us a clue as to the time of year that this invasion will occur! Continuing with the "Exodus" parallel, if the invasion were to occur just before Passover—the time of the original "Exodus"—then there would be exactly seven months until Yom Kippur. Because Israel will undergo a spiritual awakening due to this divine deliverance, that may motivate her to cleanse the land prior to this spiritually meaningful Day of Atonement—Yom Kippur. Another hint that this may be a spring invasion is that God invites the birds to feast on the dead. The large, European birds of prey—the raptors—migrate through Israel only in the spring and fall.

This milestone, in addition to being a treacherous Russian act, is also a judgment of God. It is God Himself who is setting the hook in the Russian jaw. Russia and her radical Moslem allies will meet their doom on the mountains of Israel. As a result of that judgment, God will reveal Himself to both the nations and to Israel.

> With pestilence and with blood I shall enter into judgment with him; and I shall rain on him, and on his troops, and on the many peoples who are with him, a torrential rain, with hailstones, fire, and brimstone. And I shall magnify Myself, sanctify Myself, and make Myself known in the sight of many nations; and they will know that I am the Lord (Ezekiel 38:22,23).

> I shall set My glory among the nations; and all the nations will see My judgment which I have executed, and My hand which I have laid on them. And the house of Israel will know that I am the Lord their God from that day onward (Ezekiel 39:21,22).

As the result of God's destruction of the invading force, the world will know that the God of Israel is the one and only true God. But it also allows room for us to ponder some interesting questions:

> How will this affect the faith of Israel's Moslem neighbors? Is this the time of Egypt's conversion from Islam to Judaism? (Isaiah 19:21).

> Is the "glory" which is set among the nations here referring to the return of the

Shekinah glory? Is this the time when the visible sign of God's presence returns to the holy of holies?

How will the evil prince take the news that he was not called to defend Israel (as per the terms of the Middle East Peace Covenant), but her God was? Will he be brazen enough to claim credit for himself? Will he use Israel's divine deliverance as a messianic credential?

To summarize, the Russo-Israeli war will be—

• initiated by a coalition of forces led by Russia;

• borne of hatred and envy of Israel; and

• used by God to reveal Himself as the protector of His people.

According to Revelation 20:7-10, at the end of the millennium there will be another war against another Israeli government—Messiah's government. The mastermind behind this plot will be none other than Satan himself. Those whom he deceives into joining in the war with him are symbolically called Gog and Magog, in order to draw a parallel to the invasion we have just discussed. And just as God will utterly destroy the Russian-led armies, so God will likewise destroy the satanically led rebels.

The Kingdom of the Evil Prince

A great body of the prophetic Word is devoted to describing living conditions during the seven-year period of the Covenant. That time is often referred to as the "tribulation." The second half of the Covenant's term is referred to as "the great tribulation" or "the time of Jacob's trouble."[15] During this 3½-year period, people will not only be faced with God's judgment in the form of natural catastrophes, but they will be ruled by the most hateful and oppressive dictatorship this world has ever seen.

The prophets have described this dictatorship—"the kingdom of the evil prince"—at great length. Let's look at some of the general characteristics of this kingdom:

♦ *The Kingdom Is European-Based*

Daniel tells us that this kingdom will grow out of Europe.[16] This is implied when he tells us that its dictator, the evil prince, will be from the people who destroyed the city and the sanctuary.[17] We know from history that Jerusalem and the temple were destroyed by the armies of Europe, led by Rome, in 70 A.D. In addition, prophetic visions of this beastly kingdom described it as arising from the sea.[18] This may be descriptive of Europe's relative geographic position to Israel—that is, across the Mediterranean Sea.

♦ *This European Kingdom Rules the World*

This kingdom is not content to restrict its rule to its own geographic borders. Rather, Daniel tells us that this kingdom "will be different from all the other kingdoms, and it will devour the whole earth and tread it down and crush it."[19] This kingdom will have planetary dominion.

♦ *This Kingdom Rules Through Economic Control*

Other kingdoms have conquered their known worlds by military might, but not this European kingdom; it will be "different," for this kingdom and her evil prince will conquer with peace.[20] And how does one peacefully conquer the world, you may be asking? By economic might! In Revelation 13 we are told that the entire world stands in awe of this government; "Who can compete with these people?" they will say. That same chapter also describes a tightly controlled economic and financial system.[21] It will be a global cashless society. Anyone who wants to participate in this kingdom's marketplace and buy or sell anything will have to be a member in good standing of the prince's credit system. Security will be very tight. No more of these credit cards which can be lost or stolen. Each person will receive a number and it will be bio-implanted either on the forehead or the right hand. No bio-implant, and you will not be able to buy. No implant reader at the point of sale, and your business is closed down.

This system may be introduced to put the black marketeers, the drug lords, the tax evaders, the mob, and the money launderers out of business. Without cash or access to the master system, they would have no monetary exchange mechanism. But the same system would give the government absolute and total control of every monetary transaction. Life apart from this system will be near-impossible. People, nations, and regional economic clubs will admire the success of the system and will clamor to be part of it. But just as motivating will be the fear of being excommunicated from this global financial system, for it will "devour the whole earth."

The Prince Who Is to Come

The ruler of this kingdom will be the evil prince. He will be a charismatic European leader who arises and authors the Middle East Peace Covenant. He will appear to be a man of peace and great spiritual and diplomatic insight. He will promise that Europe will guarantee Israel's peace and spiritual freedom in exchange for the division of her land. For the next 3½ years his government will be coalescing. Revelation 13:5 tells us that it is at this point that the prince is given authority. His kingdom will now rise to its full strength.

This man will not only have pretensions, but a plan as well. He will establish a planetary management team. He will not depend upon any kind of leaders from a bygone age, but will place the administration of his kingdom in the hands of a cabinet of ten ministers.[22] Perhaps they will each be given a global region to administer, for John tells us that they shall "receive authority as kings."[23] The prince's newly found authority will feed his latent megalomania and he will become an autocratic monster.

I believe we can see this transformation from benign to malignant power in the language of Revelation 13. This passage pulls no punches; the prince's kingdom is here referred to as a beast, and his satanic mentor is referred to as a dragon. In the beginning of the chapter we read that—

> the whole earth was amazed and followed after
> the beast; and they worshiped the dragon,
> because he gave his authority to the beast;
> and they worshiped the beast, saying, "Who is
> like the beast, and who is able to wage war
> with him?" (Revelation 13:3,4).

It would therefore appear that early in the prince's reign this worship is volitional and genuine. But then there is an abrupt change. Later in the same chapter we are introduced to a second beast, similar to a cabinet chief. We are told that the second beast "exercises all the authority of the first beast in his presence. And he *makes* the earth and those who dwell in it to worship the first beast" (v. 12). We have a sudden transformation from awestruck, volitional worship to compulsion!

How will this megalomania manifest itself? In the middle of the term of the Middle East Peace Covenant the evil prince will turn on Israel. No longer will he be the guarantor of Israel's peace, but of her persecution. Perhaps he will be in a blind rage because Israel turned to God as He saved her from the Russian-led invasion instead of relying on the prince's Covenant with them.

What motivation could precipitate such a swing in behavior from being a champion of peace to being a champion of death? Perhaps his new authority will go to his head. Certainly his empowerment by Satan will affect his behavior. We can only imagine what thoughts may go through his head:

> Three-and-a-half years ago I made a Covenant
> with the Israelis. For $3^1/2$ years I have made it
> possible for them and the rest of the world to
> live in relative peace. When the Russians and
> Moslems invaded recently, did they turn to me
> for help? No! They turned back to their mysti-
> cism, and called on their God. Did he give

them peace in the last 2000 years? No, I did. Now their enemies have been defeated through some "miracle." Not only is Israel attributing their salvation to their God, but so is the whole world.

For 3½ years the world has looked to me for leadership and hope. I am trying to save mankind and usher in a golden age. We are so close! But now my authority is being called into question, and I will soon lose control. I've got to think of something, and fast. . . . Yes! I've got it! Where's my cabinet chief? Pack your "miracle bag"—we're off to Jerusalem for the performance of our lives!

Perhaps as a pure act of megalomania, or perhaps as a face-saving gesture by which he could claim credit for Israel's supernatural salvation, the prince will commit an abominable act. He will fly to Jerusalem and enter the newly constructed holy of holies. There in the temple of God he will sit down, enthroning himself and declaring himself to be God.[24] In Revelation 11:8 Jerusalem is mystically called Sodom and Egypt, perhaps denoting its desecrated state. When this desecration occurs, Jesus offered some advice to those who are in Israel at that time:

Therefore when you see the Abomination of Desolation which was spoken of through Daniel the prophet, standing in the holy place (let the reader understand), then let those who are in Judea flee to the mountains; let him who is on the housetop not go down to get the things out that are in his house; and let him who is in the field not turn back to get his cloak. But woe to those who are with child and to those who nurse babes in those days! But pray that

your flight may not be in the winter or on the
Sabbath; for then there will be a great tribulation, such as has not occurred since the
beginning of the world until now, nor ever
shall (Matthew 24:15-21).

In Jerusalem, the prince and his cabinet chief will
perform "miracles" in order to authenticate the prince's
divine credentials. The Israelis will not be an easy audi-
ence. Then, as has been the case for the last 2500 years,
Israel will once again be pursued. She will flee into the
mountainous wilderness. As Daniel has prophesied, biblical temple service will cease.

While the prince will be gathering power during the
first half of the Covenant, God will station "two wit-
nesses" in the streets of Jerusalem. They will prophesy,
call down God's judgments, and consume their enemies
with fire. They will make the prince's life miserable for
$3^{1}/_{2}$ years.[25] When they have finished their 42-month
testimony, the prince, having set up his throne in Jerusalem, will have them executed. Their bodies will be left
in the street for worldwide public viewing. Perhaps CNN
will provide live coverage. After $3^{1}/_{2}$ days they will be
resurrected and Jerusalem will be hit by a devastating
earthquake as the prince's acts of murder are immediately judged by God.

God's people will be oppressed, hunted down, and
martyred, judgments will be rained down and divine
records will be kept.

The prince will put down all rebellions and will rule
harshly. He and his henchmen will put in place a worldwide economic system which allows them to totally
control commerce down to the grass roots level. Their
society will exclude everyone who does not have an
approved cashless account. Because of the importance of
that account to daily existence and to protect it from

theft, account information will be bio-implanted, leaving a small mark on the hand or temple.

I suppose if this system were to be massively and globally boycotted, the prince would never be able to achieve real control of the planet. But most people and businesses will happily comply. Perhaps this is why collusion with this system of control constitutes automatic exclusion from the coming messianic kingdom. Those will be days of hard choices—between eating and eternal life. Those will be days of divine judgment, persecution, death, and destruction on an unprecedented scale. And when humanity is at its lowest point, the rumors will start to circulate among Messiah's followers: "There's going to be a coup!" The inspirational word will be secretly passed: "Cheer up; hold fast! There's good news—Messiah is coming!"

Armageddon and the Advent of Messiah

While some of the milestones we have discussed so far may be only vaguely familiar to some readers, the one that undoubtedly has the highest recognition factor is Armageddon. However, this is also the event that is the most widely misunderstood. For most people the word "Armageddon" connotes "the end of the world." But this is not the biblical teaching.

Armageddon is not the end of the *world* but the end of a pernicious *world order*. Armageddon is the final struggle between the armies of the evil prince and the armies of Messiah. God's purpose is not the destruction of the planet. God's purpose is to reestablish His creation as He originally intended it—a holy kingdom of peace and divine fellowship.

For seven years prior to Armageddon, Israel's God and His agents will have been the source of untold grief on a world scale. God's judgments will have—

- caused war, famine, pestilence, animal attacks, and earthquakes;
- burned one-third of the earth, including trees and grass;
- destroyed one-third of sea life and ships;
- reduced sun and moon light by one-third;
- killed one-third of mankind.

Of course the peoples of the world will have deserved the judgment to which they have been subject. People will continue to commit crimes against God and their neighbor without remorse.

> The rest of mankind, who were not killed by these plagues, did not repent of the works of their hands, so as not to worship demons, and the idols of gold and of silver and of brass and of stone and of wood, which can neither see nor hear nor walk; and they did not repent of their murders nor of their sorceries nor of their immorality nor of their thefts (Revelation 9:20,21).

These people will know that they deserve judgment, but they just won't want to "take their medicine." Rather than change their ways, they will strike out at the source of their affliction.

Leading this angry and vindictive global mob will be the evil prince. The judgments which will beset the earth and their Author will not escape the notice of this prince. He will have planned a peaceful world dictatorship, but then Israel's God will have challenged his power. Despite his 3½ years of occupation of God's headquarters on earth, Jerusalem, things will only get worse for the prince. He will be ready for a fight to the finish, for he knows what lies ahead.

Then the word will spread. What was only whispered in secret will then be proclaimed in the streets: Messiah is coming! Although there has been talk of Messiah's coming for millennia, now there will be unmistakable signs in the sky. These signs will herald the ultimate challenge to the prince's power.

The prince will try to focus the world's anger on a common enemy. He will prepare a "welcoming party" for Messiah in Jerusalem, sending invitations to the armies of the world. The nations, hostile and devastated by God's judgments, will eagerly respond to the call. They will assemble on the plain of Megiddo, and at the appointed time the armies will encircle Jerusalem. In addition to enjoying the opportunity to strike out at Jerusalem and her God, the nations may also attempt to find a window of opportunity to get some licks in at the dictatorial prince as well. Hopes will be high. If they can only remember the tried-and-true diplomatic and military tactics of encirclement learned during the Gulf War, there will surely be another rout!

Just as God will "hook" Russia and drag her down to Israel for judgment, now the world will be "reeled in" as well. God tells us three specific reasons for this cataclysmic judgment:

- ✦ The world's treatment of His people, particularly the captivity of the Jews (Joel 3:2,3).
- ✦ The world's division of Eretz Yisrael (The land of Israel) (Joel 3:2,3).
- ✦ Mankind's destruction of the earth (Revelation 11:18).

The battle will begin before Messiah arrives. The prince's "coalition forces" will have initial success, for Jerusalem will be placed under martial law and its occupants brutalized.

I will gather all the nations against Jerusalem
to battle, and the city will be captured, the
houses plundered, the women ravished, and
half of the city exiled, but the rest of the people
will not be cut off from the city. Then the Lord
will go forth and fight against those nations,
as when He fights on a day of battle (Zechariah 14:2,3).

Turning Point

Then the battle will be joined: Messiah arrives with
his "holy ones"![26] Strengthened by God, the "clans of
Judah" will first defeat the surrounding armies on the
"left" and "right," then the residents of Jerusalem will
retake the city as they showcase great acts of heroism.
Then God will focus His attention on the remaining
armies. At the end of the day Israel will stand alone, her
enemies divinely defeated once again.

In that day I will make the clans of Judah like
a firepot among pieces of wood and a flaming
torch among sheaves, so they will consume on
the right hand and on the left all the surrounding peoples, while the inhabitants of
Jerusalem again dwell on their own sites in
Jerusalem. The Lord also will save the tents of
Judah first in order that the glory of the house
of David and the glory of the inhabitants
of Jerusalem may not be magnified above
Judah. In that day the Lord will defend the
inhabitants of Jerusalem, and the one who is
feeble among them in that day will be like
David, and the house of David will be like God,
like the angel of the Lord before them. And it
will come about in that day that I will set

about to destroy all the nations that come against Jerusalem (Zechariah 12:6-9).

When God turns to destroy the nations, the description that Zechariah provides almost sounds like a nuclear blast.

> Now this will be the plague with which the Lord will strike all the peoples who have gone to war against Jerusalem; their flesh will rot while they stand on their feet, and their eyes will rot in their sockets, and their tongue will rot in their mouth.... So also like this plague will be the plague on the horse, the mule, the camel, the donkey, and all the cattle that will be in those camps. (Zechariah 14:12,15).

Then the evil prince and his cabinet chief will be seized, summarily judged, and thrown alive into the lake of fire.[27]

Then Messiah Jesus will become King Jesus. As one of his first royal acts, He will sit upon His throne and judge the nations.[28] He separates these survivors into three groups:

- ◆ His brothers—those who have faithfully followed Him during the seven years of judgment, both Jew and Gentile.

- ◆ Those who have given comfort to His brothers. While His brothers were being economically strangled by the prince's economic management system, these people will have shared food, drink, clothing, shelter, and compassion with them. Their outward demonstration of compassion is evidence of their inward acceptance of Messiah. These people King Jesus will welcome into His kingdom.

◆ Those who have not given comfort to his
brothers. These will be people who either
through cowardice or malevolence have committed sins of both omission and commission
against his brothers. When they saw them in
need, they will have either turned away or
turned them in to the authorities. These
people King Jesus will condemn. They will
face the same punishment as the prince with
whom they conspired.

Israel and her God will have triumphed! Her Messiah
and King will have come! And when the people of Israel
see Him, there will be a flash of recognition. It is
Yeshua—Jesus—the rejected one, the crucified one. It
is the one whose Greek name, Jesus, was used by the
blasphemous Gentiles as an excuse to kill Jews for millennia. The words of the psalmist will then be recalled:

My God, my God, why has Thou forsaken me?
Far from my deliverance are the words of my
groaning.... But I am a worm, and not a man,
a reproach of men, and despised by the people.
All who see me sneer at me; they separate
with the lip, they wag the head, saying, "Commit yourself to the Lord; let Him deliver him;
Let Him rescue him, because He delights in
him.".... A band of evildoers has encompassed
me; they pierced my hands and my feet" (Psalm
22:1,6-8,16).

At that point the Jewish nation will lament.

I will pour out on the house of David and on the
inhabitants of Jerusalem the Spirit of grace
and of supplication, so that they will look on
Me whom they have pierced; and they will

> mourn for Him, as one mourns for an only son,
> and they will weep bitterly over Him, like the
> bitter weeping over a firstborn (Zechariah
> 12:10).

Great will be the lament of Israel! For two millennia
they will have been separated from this their beloved
Son. Initially their fathers rejected this man, Yeshua,
and His messianic credentials. Then this separation
was made near-irrevocable by the Gentiles. First they
obscured his identity with pagan tradition, then they
murdered Jews in "Jesus' name." But all this will become ancient history, for Messiah will transform their
mourning through forgiveness:

> Shout for joy, O daughter of Zion! Shout in
> triumph, O Israel! Rejoice and exult with all
> your heart, O daughter of Jerusalem! The
> Lord has taken away His judgments against
> you, He has cleared away your enemies. The
> King of Israel, the Lord, is in your midst; you
> will fear disaster no more (Zephaniah 3:14,15).

Israel will rejoice! After 6000 years of promise, her
Messiah will have come to rule and to reign. Having
defeated His enemies and judged His captives, He will
then turn to the business of establishing His kingdom.
Armageddon is not the end of the world, but a new
beginning!

The Messianic Kingdom

Beyond Armageddon, the nations will be judged and
the messianic kingdom will begin. Jesus the King will
ascend His throne to rule and reign as King of Kings. His
reign will be characterized by universal peace, holiness,

and justice, and it will last for a thousand years.[29] This will be an age of true peace, not the simulated variety provided by the evil prince.

In those days the house of the Lord will be rebuilt and rededicated on Mount Moriah in Jerusalem. God has provided the detailed plans for that temple in Ezekiel chapters 40 to 43. It will be a beautiful sight! A new order of sacrifice will be instituted as prescribed by God in Ezekiel 45.

Jerusalem's new temple will not only be *Israel's* center of worship, but the center of worship for the *whole world*. People from all over the world will go to the house of the Lord to learn how to lead righteous lives. The nations will seek out the company of the Jewish people because of their special relationship with God. Jerusalem will also become the center of international law and justice. International conflict will forever cease as King Jesus arbitrates the differences between peoples.[30]

And who are the subjects and administrators of this kingdom? They will be the faithful followers of Messiah throughout the ages—some resurrected, some translated at the rapture, some who have survived the kingdom of the evil prince. These subjects can be divided into the following groups:

♦ The Resurrected

Those Resurrected at the Rapture

This group includes those who died in their faith from Adam until the rapture. It also includes those of us who are faithful and living at the time of the rapture. All will be raised to immortality at the rapture. This group is part of Messiah's bride, who will live in the New Jerusalem.[31] These faithful ones will have spent the seven years of the

Covenant with Messiah, shielded from the storms of judgment.

The Faithful Who Died During the Seven-Year Covenant

This group includes those who find faith in Messiah after the rapture and who die before the establishment of the kingdom. Some may have been murdered because of their faith and their refusal to be "marked" by the evil prince.[32] The spirits of these faithful ones will join the Messiah in the New Jerusalem until the kingdom comes. When the kingdom is established, they will be resurrected.

♦ **The Tribulation Survivors**

This group includes those who find faith in Messiah or support His followers. When Messiah judges the nations, these men and women will have been found worthy to enter His kingdom. These men and women will retain their mortality and procreate until they too are transformed to immortality at the beginning of the eternal kingdom.

We as Christians belong to the first major group—the soon-to-be raptured followers of Messiah. We will reign and rule[33] with Jesus from our regal city. We, the bride of Messiah, will be the occupants of the heavenly New Jerusalem.[34] And a beautiful and great city it will be:

♦ It is a holy city that exists in the heavens until it descends to the new earth in the eternal kingdom.

♦ It is brilliant due to the physical presence of the glory of God, and its brilliance illuminates the entire new earth.

♦ It has a high wall which contains 12 gates named after the 12 tribes of Israel and each made of a single pearl.

♦ Its wall is built upon 12 foundation stones named after Messiah's 12 apostles and each adorned with semiprecious stones.

♦ It is cubical, measuring 1500 miles on each side, and both the city and its streets are made of pure gold.

Administration of the Kingdom

Jesus will be the King of Kings. Reporting directly to Him will be a subordinate group of rulers. Some interpreters believe that Israel itself will be administered by the resurrected King David himself.[35]

Contrary to popular belief, we will not be sitting idly playing harps and lining up to get fitted for "angelic wings." Instead, we will be a separated kingdom of priests and kings.[36] A parable found in Luke 19:12-27 indicates that we may be given areas to administer and judge. The apostle Paul encourages us to exercise the gift of discernment and wisdom in our daily walk in preparation for our coming duties. First Corinthians 6:1-3 indicates that these administrative portfolios will include sitting in judgment of angels:

Does any one of you, when he has a case against his neighbor, dare to go to law before the unrighteous, and not before the saints [Messiah's followers]? Or do you not know that the saints will judge the world? And if the

> world is judged by you, are you not competent
> to constitute the smallest law courts? Do you
> not know that we shall judge angels? How
> much more, the matters of this life?

It seems we will be kept very busy reviewing cases, judging our citizenry, and making wise administrative decisions.

The second major group of people, the tribulation survivors, are the countless numbers of faithful men and women who will make it through the seven years alive. They will not worship the prince and receive his mark. This group is comprised of both Jews and righteous Gentiles and those who had compassion upon "Messiah's brothers" during the oppressive reign of the evil prince. They are not resurrected but are physically and spiritually much as we are today. Having survived the kingdom of the blasphemous prince, they will now be governed by the kingdom of the Prince of Peace.

After almost three millennia of persecution at Gentile hands, Messiah's Jewish subjects will be elevated to the position of the premier citizens of the kingdom.

> You will be called the priests of the Lord; you
> will be spoken of as ministers of our God. You
> will eat the wealth of nations, and in their
> riches you will boast. Instead of your shame
> you will have a double portion, and instead of
> humiliation they will shout for joy over their
> portion. Therefore they will possess a double
> portion in their land; everlasting joy will be
> theirs (Isaiah 61:6,7).

Jews will still be sought after, but this time with humility and to act as advocates for the Gentiles with the Lord:

> "Many peoples and mighty nations will come
> to seek the Lord of hosts in Jerusalem and to

entreat the favor of the Lord." Thus says the Lord of hosts, "In those days ten men from all the nations will grasp the garment of a Jew saying, 'Let us go with you, for we have heard that God is with you.'" (Zechariah 8:22,23).

The kingdom will be the perfect environment.

* Satan will be removed, so there will be no supernatural temptation.

* The curse will be lifted from the earth; it will bear fruit abundantly, and animals will dwell in peace.

* The rulers and judgments will be just and fair.

* Mortal subjects will continue to tend their crops and flocks, build their houses, bake their bread, and reproduce; they will live to ages much older than now.[37]

All in all, it will be a "back-to-Eden" experience, with one small difference. These mortal subjects will still have a sin-prone nature. Even though they are living in a perfect environment, they will still sin and rebel. This is why we are told that Jesus will rule with a rod of iron.[38] Their compliance with kingdom rules will not always be volitional. As administrators, we will have our work cut out for us.

After the thousand years are complete, Satan will be loosed. He will again deceive mortal man and organize a rebellion.[39] Man's sin-prone nature will be put to the test one final time, and again many people will fail. This rebellion will be very similar to the Russo-Israeli War. This is why these gathering rebels are called Gog and Magog.[40] But this war will end as the other, with the Lord's enemies totally destroyed.[41]

The Eternal Kingdom

Beyond Armageddon and beyond the messianic kingdom is the eternal kingdom of God.[42] At this point the faithful mortals of the messianic kingdom will be resurrected to eternal life. Then, prior to the establishment of the eternal kingdom, two judgments will take place. First, the dead who have rejected Messiah and His substitutionary death will be judged according to their works. Those who are judged guilty of breaking God's law—and all have done so—will be condemned and separated from God for all eternity. Second, the heavens and earth will be purged with fire. Our worn and tattered heaven and earth will pass away.

> The day of the Lord will come like a thief, in which the heavens will pass away with a roar and the elements will be destroyed with intense heat, and the earth and its works will be burned up (2 Peter 3:10).

Then there will be a new creation—a new heaven and a new earth. Mankind will have a new beginning with his Creator. God and man will be physically reunited. The New Jerusalem, the habitation of God and Messiah's bride-queen, will descend from heaven to the earth. There God will dwell with His people throughout all eternity.

> Behold, the tabernacle of God is among men, and He shall dwell among them, and they shall be His people, and God Himself shall be among them (Revelation 21:3).

The millennial temple and its new order of sacrifice will pass away with the old earth. This new creation will not have or need a temple, because God will dwell among His people. His glory, the Shekinah glory, will be their light; there will be no more sun or moon, day or night.

All people of faith will have been resurrected and spiritually perfected. There will be no more cowardice, faithlessness, wickedness, or hatred. All sources of sorrow and misery will also pass away. There will be no more death or grieving, no more crying or pain. God and man will be united and will dwell forever in perfect peace. All creation will be recast according to the Creator's original plan.

Beloved friend, there are joyous adventures ahead for those whose trust is in the Lord! Before we embark on our discussion of the pathways that will lead the world to these milestones, take a moment to assess your account with God. Have you allowed Jesus the Messiah to make payment for your sin? If you haven't, why not talk to Him about it now? If you have, are you being faithful to Him, living "in peace, spotless and blameless"? Are you desiring His coming as a bride desires her groom and her wedding day?

Let us each pray that we might be found worthy of our beloved Lord, Bridegroom, and coming King, Messiah Jesus!

3

INTRIGUING
DETOURS

Two ancient pathways are in the process of taking dramatic turns—the pathways of *government* and *power*. They are very important because they underlie and foundationally support our world as we know it. When they begin to twist and turn, this has the same geopolitical effect on our world as the collision of unseen seismic plates has a physical effect. The torquing of these pathways is the root source for many of the more visible collisions of peoples and nations.

The section of the pathway of government upon which we have walked these past several centuries is marked "Nation-State." This is a system of government in which the largest denomination of power is in the form of *nations*. While some borders may shift as the result of local squabbles, and the names of some nations appear to come with periodic expiration dates, this basic geographic unit of measure has been immutable for almost a millennium.

We are now on the verge of witnessing a fundamental change in the way geography is denominated. When this metamorphosis takes place, the face of the world that we live in will be quite different.

The pathway of government is turning away from the

nation-state system, and is now headed toward *world governance.* Today, people increasingly view national sovereignty as an obstacle to universal peace and prosperity. This dream of peace, coupled with the planetary scope of the problems encountered in the late twentieth century, is causing the pathway of government to be detoured from the nation-state to world government. We will examine how this detour may be the turn in the path which leads us to the final form of world government described in the Bible.

The section of the pathway of power on which most of us in the West have walked is marked "Democracy." Democracy can be defined as a system of order in which the ultimate power rests in the hands of the people. In recent years this section of the pathway had been broadening as more and more nations pursued democracy as a universal form of government. As Communism has collapsed worldwide, democracy has been billed as the only viable ideology. But as governments have attempted to actually implement democratic reform, they have been frustrated. The steps before us on the pathway of power appear to be headed in the direction of monarchy. When we think of monarchy today, we think of regal figureheads who reign but do not rule. Such mere figureheads wield only as much influence as you or I on national policy. In our discussion here I want you to think about monarchy in its literal sense: "mono-archy," rule by one individual. As people the world over become increasingly desperate and frightened of the future, they are going to be looking for an omnipotent paternal figure. The world's frustration with national bureaucrats, the intractability of the world's problems, and a childish desire that "Daddy fix!" will open the door for monarchy. We will examine how this turn in the path may directly lead to the reign of the evil prince.

The Pathway of Government

Decline of the Nation-State System

Before we begin discussing the fall of the nation-state system, we need to see how the world has arrived at the point where we stand today.

Between the fourth and fifth centuries A.D., Rome collapsed under the onslaught of fierce Germanic tribes from the north. This was the end of European central government. Europe was subsequently governed by countless local Germanic kings and feudal lords. These kings were relatively weak, and their power was limited to the borders of their own estates. Kings extended their influence by persuading other feudal lords to pledge allegiance and military support to them. Many of these lords were militarily stronger than the king himself, which created a very volatile atmosphere.

Power dramatically shifted from this diverse network of "feudal allegiance" to a strong central monarchy after the Crusades (1095-1291). Many of the feudal lords had died in combat. It was also at this time that kings gained access to gunpowder and could breach the walls of an errant lord's realm. The emerging merchant class supported the king because they were very anxious to see central control over a geographically expanded realm so that their property and trade routes would be protected.

By the sixteenth and seventeenth centuries, these absolute monarchs became a mystical symbol of national identity. Occasionally the king became the symbol of a people who had a common language, history, customs, and body of law. But more often he became the rallying point of ethnically diverse peoples who were geographically related and who shared a common vision of the future. Ethnic differences were put aside as people gained pride in their new national identity represented by the king.

This was the evolution of the nation-state. It is hard for those of us who have grown up during its heyday to imagine any other system.

Today, however, the reduced need for a strong national defense and national identity is being counterbalanced by a growing need for ethnic identity. An article in the *New York Times* of June 24, 1990, reports that we are "... in an era when nationalisms are fragmenting rather than enlarging geographical domains. But a process, however tenuous and exploratory, of rediscovering old cultural, historical, religious and commercial bonds is under way...."[1]

Removal of the threat of war is leading people to consider redesigning their governments to suit their local ethnic concerns. This movement is further fueled by the worldwide embrace of democracy. "At long last the idea that governments should exist to serve the governed, not vice versa, is gaining the upper hand. The logic of this idea is that people would not only choose the men and women who will temporarily rule them but also the units in which they will be ruled."[2]

The death knell appears to be tolling for the nation-state. For many centuries the political boundaries of a nation were drawn by conquest and treaty. As ethnicity becomes a more potent force in shaping the world of the future, nations that have politically drawn borders rather than ethnic borders will be plagued by civil unrest. Canada and the Soviet Union have been prime examples: "... Canada and the Soviet Union, despite their many differences, have one thing in common: they are countries moulded by conquest, not by consent."[3]

Unfortunately, political borders are more the rule than the exception: "Of the countries round the world, rather few are neatly filled by single nations. Japan, yes, and France too.... But for the most part countries and nations are a mismatch: millions of Hungarians outside Hungary, millions of Chinese outside China (or

Taiwan), a million Turks inside Bulgaria, millions of Irish in the United Kingdom. Some countries, such as India, Nigeria and Yugoslavia, contain a wonderfully diverse cocktail of nations. And some nations—the Basques, the Kurds, the Palestinians and the Cree Indians—have no country at all.

"None of this would matter but for nationalism. But nationalism ... is an enduring phenomenon, and one that looks more enduring than the map of the world as it is drawn in the late twentieth century. Most of the countries on that map owe their shape to the collapse of the Ottoman, Hapsburg, French and British empires. Fueled by the fires of self-determination, and made economically self-confident by the prospect of regional cooperation, lots of those countries look set to break up again."[4]

There will of course be exceptions to the dissolution of the nation-state. Those countries like Japan, France, and others whose national boundaries are coincident with their ethnic boundaries should survive.[5] It is also interesting that the *Economist* believes that the U.S.A. will survive intact: "... the United States has succeeded better than any other in making a nation out of an utterly heterogeneous mix of peoples.... The ideology of Americanism should be strong enough to hold the United States together."[6]

The Role of the United Nations

Although the United Nations is thought of as a "globalist" organization, in fact it is not. Rather, it is a loose confederation of sovereign nation-states. When successful, it controls the competing interests of its member states. As the nation-state declines, what role can we expect that the United Nations will play?

It is possible that before being totally eclipsed by the coming European World Government, the U.N. may yet have its day in the sun. This could happen if a strong Secretary General appears and provides true leadership to the U.N. Perhaps he could, through strength of will, convince the members of the Security Council to continue to act in unison. Perhaps the U.N. could be restructured by the industrialized West into a truly "global government."

There is a remote possibility that the evil prince could begin his career at the U.N. before moving on to Europe. Perhaps he could fill the position of Secretary General sometime fairly soon. There is even talk of changing the term of office from five to *seven* years. If you see the U.N. becoming involved with the negotiation of the Middle East Peace Covenant, and the lead negotiator is a European, keep an eye on that man.

However, the likelihood of this happening is not too great, for these reasons:

- The position of Secretary General will probably be filled with a weak, compromise candidate. This will be particularly true if the selection process continues to select the most mutually agreeable candidate from a targeted geographic area, rather than scouring the globe for a person with the best global leadership potential.

- If the military and Communist hard-liners again flex their muscles in Moscow, the Cold War may be renewed. Anything short of total agreement between Moscow and Washington in the Security Council spells U.N. paralysis.

- The CSCE (Conference on Security and Co-operation in Europe) includes all of Europe, the U.S.A., Canada, and the former Soviet Union. It now has a bureaucracy called a "secretariat" and has been chartered as a "dispute settlement organization." This role appears to duplicate that of the U.N., but it only includes the nations from the first and second world. Like the U.N., the first and second world "pay for it"; but unlike the U.N., the first and second world "own" the CSCE.

As tensions grow between the third world and the industrialized nations, dependence may shift to the CSCE for dispute resolution between members. Third-world nations which step out of line, not having a voice in the CSCE, could face an iron fist.

The industrialized nations will be very happy to shut out third-world meddling and whining. The third world believes that the United Nations Security Council is controlled by the West. They point to the bribery, threats, arm-twisting, and lobbying in which the United States engaged in order to coerce the Security Council membership to vote for the resolutions against Iraq. Long after the Gulf crisis is forgotten, the Security Council will still be viewed with suspicion by the third world.

The West, which bankrolls the U.N., resents third-world domination of the General Assembly and the U.N. bureaucracy. In the General Assembly, the tiniest nation has the same voting weight as the largest nation. In addition, it is often held hostage by third-world issues that are of little interest to the industrialized West. Just as U.N. activity in the Gulf War will leave bitterness in the third world, the West will have lingering suspicions about third-world judgment and its commitment to peace. For as the West was attempting to bring down the regime of a dictator it likened to Hitler, third-world nations in various parts of the world were declaring their support for him. That these nations were able to

overlook Saddam Hussein's atrocities bears testimony
to the third world's intense hatred for the West. Will the
West be able to trust the future judgments of these
nations as they sit together at the U.N.?

The West has pressed for structural reform and account-
ability at the U.N., but to little avail. Alan Keyes, former
assistant secretary of state for international organization
affairs, was recently interviewed by *Insight* magazine.

> Keyes says strict enforcement of budget reform
> is the only cure for the United Nations' bu-
> reaucratic blight and increasingly demanding
> voting blocs of less developed countries, whose
> own budget contributions are minimal. "There
> must be a balance between those countries
> that foot the bill and those that have the
> majority of votes" to ensure financial respon-
> sibility, he says. Delegates of Third World
> countries have long campaigned for greater
> representation in high-level posts, while de-
> veloped countries protest that those who con-
> tribute the majority of funding should have a
> greater voice in deciding how their money is
> spent. The growing strength of the developing
> bloc was demonstrated in late October when
> Perez de Cuellar appointed his private office
> chief, Virandra Dayal of India, to head the
> U.N. High Commission for Refugees, an agency
> responsible for the support of the world's
> 15 million refugees, with a 1990 budget of
> $378 million. Perez de Cuellar crowned Dayal
> without consulting delegates of the indus-
> trialized countries that provide the bulk of the
> commission's funding.[7]

Mismanagement, inefficiency, inequity, and unre-
solved conflicts between nations will hasten the decline

of the United Nations and perhaps shift its dispute resolution responsibilities to the CSCE.

Two-Tiered Government of the Future

The pathway of government is turning away from the nation-state system and toward a two-tiered world government—global and local. At the global level there will likely be a world federation of regional organizations. At the local level there will be countless ethnic states. The *Economist* has reported that—

> flag makers and cartographers can now look forward to a new redrawing of boundaries across the globe. This time the new shapes will appear at two levels: on high, in an acronymic stratosphere where people's lives are run not by national governments but by regional groupings of ECs, CSCEs, ACCs, NAFTAs and the like; and down below, in a basement world of Eritreas, Tamil, Eelams and Uzbekistans.[8]

An example of a two-tiered system appeared in the June 24, 1990, issue of the *New York Times*:

> Cene [Italy], a small valley town in Lombardy near the foothills of the Alps, stands in the front ranks of a young and increasingly potent regional party called the Lombard League, led by people who are fed up with domination by Rome. In effect, they insist on creating a United States of Italy, a federal system that might be patterned less on an American model than the Swiss, but either way would give full autonomy to Lombardy and other regions in the country's affluent North. . . . Under the league's

federal plan, Rome would take whatever small
share of tax money it may need for national
defense and foreign policy. The rest would stay
where it is collected.[9]

In this example, the two tiers are currently envisioned at a local and national level. However, Italy
is part of the European Community, which is itself
attempting to build the very federal system that the
Lombards seek. As soon as the EC federal government is
in place, the midlevel Italian national government envisioned by the Lombards would be redundant.

The ethnic state's purpose will be to provide for the
operational needs of the local community: "... not all
issues rise naturally to such lofty heights. Left to themselves, some sink to local level, where government and
governed can keep easily in touch, the better to sort out
their difficulties over education, transport, housing,
health and even taxation. This is the case for 'subsidiary'—that is promoted by the European Commission in
Brussels."[10]

In addition, ethnic states will ensure the survival of
local culture.

As the Lombard League has expressed, "We want to
impart a culture... not a subculture."[11]

The Top Tier

The top tier of government will be a global federation
of regional organizations. Indeed, regional organizations are rapidly taking shape, the most notable being
the European Community, or more broadly, the proposed
European Union. The important issue here is that mankind has begun to recognize the benefits of supranational government. The *Economist* has reported:

Countries are getting together now as never before for good reasons.... As economies become more interlinked, so their people prosper. Single markets bring doubled returns.... Many of today's noneconomic problems can best be tackled internationally. Unilateral action by, say, Sweden to contain emission of nasty gases ... will be of little value; concerted action is required. Drugs, defense, terrorism all demand intervention beyond the boundaries of any one country. More cooperation is essential.[12]

Robert Dahl in his book *Democracy and its Critics* states:

The boundaries of a country, even a country as large as the United States, are now much smaller than the boundaries of the decisions that significantly affect the fundamental interests of its citizens. A country's economic life, physical environment, national security, and survival are highly, and probably increasingly, dependent on actors and actions that are outside the country's boundaries and not directly subject to its government.... Just as the rise of the national state reduced the capacity of local residents to exercise control over matters of vital importance to them by means of their local governments, so the proliferation of transnational activities and decisions reduces the capacity of the citizens of a country to exercise control over matters vitally important to them by means of their national government. To that extent, the governments of countries are becoming local

governments.... In my judgment for the fore-
seeable future transnational forces will continue to erode national autonomy....[13]

Many of today's thinkers are looking to the European
Community (EC) to be the model for future world government. At one level, the EC will be cloned to create
other regional organizations of a similar nature. On a
second level, the EC is becoming the model and the test
bed for world government itself.

The experiment currently underway is in the area of
supranational monetary systems. An editorial in the
Economist spoke of the need to control and minimize the
violent swings in exchange rates called "overshooting."

> ... exchange-rate architects have to design a
> regime that minimizes the harm done by over-
> shooting. The most promising embryo is the
> European monetary system [EMS]. For a group
> of countries with few formal trade barriers
> between them, the EMS is essential. If their
> exchange rates were to move erratically, the
> Community's internal trading regime would
> not survive. It would be overwhelmed by pres-
> sure on individual governments to protect
> their industries against sudden and currency-
> driven losses of competitiveness. The EMS has
> another vital merit. At its heart is an inde-
> pendent central bank that loathes inflation....
> And it allows Europe's more slovenly coun-
> tries to lock into Teutonic rectitude on infla-
> tion, which in time produces Teutonic rewards
> in the form of lower interest rates.... The
> EMS's next task is to develop a single Euro-
> pean currency.... Ahead of a single currency,
> Europe will be building its single market. The
> free movement of goods and services, people

and capital is the complement to a common currency: that, after all, is what happens within national economies.... Once Europe has a single currency in a single economic space, its system can be copied and extended.

The desirable end to that process will be a world currency, serving a world economy in which trade and investment will be far more international than they are today. To clinch its attractiveness, the world currency will have to retain its purchasing power more successfully than any of the national or regional currencies it replaces. For that, it must be managed by an independent central bank which is charged with keeping the currency stable against the price of a basket of commodities.... Fanciful? It gets less so every day. Each bout of over-shooting brings more pain: each intervention by central banks provides less relief; each episode raises sharper questions. That pattern will not go on forever. A world currency cometh.[14]

From our discussion of the kingdom of the evil prince, we have established that his kingdom will eventually "devour the whole earth." It is probable that the prince will begin his dictatorial career as the leader of a European regional organization such as the EC. As the power of Europe grows, other regional organizations throughout the world will be voluntarily annexed. The prince's influence and authority will become global.

The resulting Global Federation will incorporate the many local governments of differing varieties: some based upon kinship ("tribes"), some based upon language ("tongues"), some based upon common culture ("nations"); some as strong as iron and some as weak as clay (Daniel 2:40-43). Truly this world federation "will be different from all the other kingdoms, and it will devour the whole earth..." (Daniel 7:23).

But before one builds up a new order one must break down the old. Nation-states are by nature protectionist, isolationist, and loath to surrender sovereignty. If the world is truly going to become one, it will have to lose the baggage of the nation-state form of government. The press has been preparing the obituary for the nation-state for many years.

It would appear that the pathway of government is veering away from the nation-state system and is leading to world government. World government may appear to be man's only hope for solving the problems of the next century—but only when God is specifically precluded from providing an alternative and better solution.

The nation-states around the world are disintegrating. This breakdown of the nation-state and the rise of two-tiered world government are strong indications that the pathway of government is approaching the milestone of the kingdom of the evil prince.

The Pathway of Power

The second pathway which is taking major twists and turns is the pathway of power. The power structure of the world is currently a broad spectrum. On one end of the scale are the democratic nations. Theoretically, the power in these countries resides with the people. On the opposite end of the scale are the nations controlled by dictatorial regimes. The power in these nations is exercised by a single man or elite body.

Communism has been viewed as the major bastion of dictatorial government. The fall of the Berlin Wall was celebrated as the symbolic fall of Communism and dictatorship. That event was hailed as the advent of a "universal democratic era." Great leaders and thinkers were quick to declare that we were witnessing an unstoppable trend toward a great, democratic, Utopian world. Democracy had triumphed!

Truly, democracy is in vogue, or at least the espousing of it. In his book *Democracy and Its Critics* Robert Dahl says, "Never in recorded history have state leaders appealed so widely to democratic ideas to legitimize their rule, even if only to justify an authoritarian government as necessary to a future transition to a true or purified democracy."[15] But in fact the fall of Communism has made the viability of a universal ideology much more likely. Given the popularity of democracy, are we entering an age where, globally, power is in the hands of the people? Absolutely not!

Roadblocks to Democracy

As the initial blush of enthusiasm began to fade, the "emerging democracies" began to realize the truth of the axiom "You can't get there from here!" Sadly, the path from Communism to democratic capitalism is basically unnavigable. Generations of Communist domination have left these nations poor, polluted, and low on personal responsibility. Freedom has little value when you are hungry and destitute.

When Communism fell and democratic reforms began to be implemented, people expected instant wealth. Instead, they received the bill for 40 to 70 years of mismanagement and their socio-economic safety nets were removed. No longer could they do a shoddy job in a state factory and be guaranteed a job and a wage. Inefficient factories were closed and massive numbers of people became unemployed. No longer could the state subsidize food staples. Prices and supplies began to fluctuate widely due to greed and inexperience with the dynamics of market economies.

When Communism fell and democratic reforms began to be implemented, people expected freedom from fear. Instead, the fear of the state security system was replaced with the fear of crime and the fear of being the object of age-old ethnic hatreds. Personal envies tear at the lives of individuals and ethnic rivalries tear at the fabric of nations themselves.

When Communism fell and democratic reforms began to be implemented, people expected that the hated bureaucrats would be tossed out on their ears. Instead, it was sadly discovered that these poorly skilled men are the best the nation had to offer. There is a distinct absence of management and organizational skills just when they are needed the most.

> The new governments of the East have discovered that the lack of institutional constraints that channel and direct and often cramp government is not so much a lack of unwanted constraint as a lack of needed institutions. Valclav Klaus, the innovative Czechoslovak finance minister, says that he has a mere handful of experts who understand what he wishes to do. Jacek Kuron, the Polish labor minister, has had to attempt to construct unemployment and social-security offices from scratch, with neither domestic blueprints nor experienced staff.[16]

If Communism has proven itself to be destitute, and the transition to democracy is too difficult to accomplish, where will these emerging democracies turn next? More than likely, they will trust their instincts and return to the system that served their ancestors well for millennia—monarchy.

Yearning for a Monarch

This yearning for a monarch was recently expressed by Yuri Shchekochikhin:

> "Russians simply are not ready for democracy," the new Parliament member complained. His constituents besieged him for help in getting jobs, or apartments, or telephones. "People here still want a good czar to fix everything," he said."[17]

This sentiment is not limited to Russia.

> If democracy does not work in Latin America, then the way is open for fundamentalist messianic leadership ... an ultranationalist rightwing movement.[18]

The perennial alternative to democracy is a system called guardianship.[19] Robert Dahl defines guardianship as "... a regime in which the state is governed by meritorious rulers who consist of a minority of adults, quite likely a very small minority, and who are not subject to the democratic process."[20] This form of government is based upon the assumption that people cannot understand or defend their own interests. Rather, their interests are best safeguarded by a small body of wise guardians. Those guardians are best qualified to rule based upon their moral understanding, their ability to achieve desirable ends, and their knowledge of the best and most efficient way to achieve those ends. Guardians are specialists in the art and science of ruling and leading.[21]

Although guardians are "morally responsible," there is no guarantee of their virtue. And unfortunately, there are no means for removing a bad guardian.[22]

History is rife with examples of bad guardianship. Robert Dahl provides us with the following counsel:

> An imperfect democracy is a misfortune for its people, but an imperfect authoritarian regime is an abomination. If prudence counsels a "max-minim" strategy—that is, choose the alternative that is the best of the worst outcomes—then the experience of the twentieth century argues powerfully against the idea of guardianship.[23]

If the world is not moving toward a Utopian democracy, is it moving toward a guardianship on a global scale as prophesied in the Bible? Mr. Dahl has made the following ominous observation:

> With respect to decisions on crucial international affairs, then, the danger is that the... [evolution of the supranational-state] will lead not to an extension of the democratic idea beyond the nation-state but to the victory in that domain of de facto guardianship.[24]

Monarchy on the Rise

Monarchy has always been a vital part of Europe, and its future looks bright. Ten constitutional monarchies have thrived in Western Europe until this day. They are in the nations of Belgium, Denmark, Liechtenstein, Luxembourg, Monaco, the Netherlands, Norway, Spain, Sweden, and the United Kingdom. The thrones of Eastern Europe flourished until earlier this century. Between 1917 and 1919 the Hohenzollerns of Germany, the Hapsburgs of Austria-Hungary, and the Romanovs of Russia lost their thrones. The growth of Communism in Eastern Europe after World War II took its toll on additional crown heads.

Today in Eastern Europe, as Communism becomes increasingly inviable and as democracy appears unattainable, monarchy is making a big comeback.

No sooner had the Berlin Wall fallen, and amongst the mass confusion and unrest which followed, Eastern Europe experienced a massive revival of monarchical sentiment, with many former subjects demonstrating for the return of their sovereign to head their downtrodden and economically impoverished nations into a new and brighter future.[25]

The following is a brief summary of some of the available thrones in Eastern Europe and their pretenders.

Throne	Pretender and Notable Quotes
Albania	King Leka, son of Zog I.
	"King Leka, though, believes that the day of liberation is drawing closer, and he envisages taking a central role. 'The monarchy is the catalyst that will permit such a change. Who has the legitimacy, the faith of the people and the national backing to act as an interim government? Only the King.'"[26]
Austria, Hungary	Otto von Hapsburg, son of Karl, the last Emperor of the Austro-Hungarian Empire and King of Hungary; represents Bavaria in the European Parliament.
	"In Hungary there is little or no chance of a Hapsburg revival. However, interest and curiosity in the would-be king, Archduke Otto Von Hapsburg, is widespread."[27]
Bulgaria	King Simeon II; reigned briefly when his father, King Boris, died in 1943. His grandfather, Ferdinand I of the Saxe-Coburg-Gotha family, was transplanted to Bulgaria from Germany, which was not well received.
	"Within days of [former Communist dictator] Zhivkov's removal, King Simeon had an historic forty-five-minute television interview in which, and in perfect Bulgarian, he addressed the nation and spoke of his exile years and of the social, cultural, political and economic problems which now confront Bulgaria.... Several political parties were formed

almost overnight to support the King and people of all ages and backgrounds began to look to King Simeon as a possible answer to the political vacuum now that the Communist party was gradually losing its grip on power.... A new era is upon Bulgaria and there is little doubt that King Simeon will return home and have a large part to play in the future of his beloved Bulgaria."[28]

Greece
: King Constantine II; reigned from 1964-1974; deposed by a military regime.

Montenegro
: Prince Nikola, great-grandson of Nikola I; will benefit if Yugoslavia splits up and Montenegro becomes sovereign again.

Romania
: King Michael; reigned two years under a Communist regime and went voluntarily into exile in 1947 rather than continue to be a Communist puppet.

"Within days of the execution of the former dictator and his wife, demonstrations of loyalty to King Michael were being being organized throughout the country, and newspapers carried articles on the Royal Family, especially concerning the unique role of the King during the war years."[29]

Russia
: Grand Duke Vladimir Kirilovich Romanov.

"Moving eastward to the Soviet Union, Gorbachev's glasnost has set free Russia's royalists, who are demanding a Romanov return. The seventy-two-year-old Grand Duke Vladimir Kirilovich Romanov, the would-be Tsar, is ready and waiting... but still refuses to apply for a visa, insisting he will only return when he is officially invited.... The Soviet Union, though, is crumbling.... The monarchy could be the only uniting force available for the Russian people.[30]

Yugoslavia
: Alexander II; chances of his return to a nation divided by ethnic strife is remote.

"In December 1988, the Crown Prince gave his first interview that was published nationwide within the country, and there has been a massive revival in monarchial sentiment ever since."[31]

Position Available: King of Europe

Perhaps the most startling "available position" is the one that may soon be opening for a European sovereign.

...the storm clouds are gathering. The meshing of Britain into Europe, both economically and legally, will inevitably dilute the influence of parliament. As a result, the authority of the monarchy will become correspondingly weaker within this loose federation of nation states. At the same time, it will become increasingly difficult for monarchy to hold the constitutional ring. The possibility of establishing a Head of State to represent the European Community is now on the political horizon. As one Brussels Eurocrat said: "There is considerable interest here in a Head of State for the European Community. It symbolizes everything the EC stands for."

While such a move is not on the immediate agenda, its very proposition does call into question the Queen's position as the Head of State of fifteen other countries beside Britain and her role as Head of the Commonwealth. "Can one person continue to sustain so many diverse roles?" asks legal historian Michael Nash, author of *A Single Europe*. It is a perfectly practical proposition to have a ceremonial Head of State for the Community. The office would be occupied on a rotating basis, rather like the European presidency. This already works effectively in Malaysia. While there is nothing in the Treaty of Rome to accommodate such a position, the pace of change in Europe now is such that I would not be surprised if what is being seriously discussed today becomes reality by the end of the decade.[32]

The creation of a head of state for the European Community may be the key to unifying the cultural diversity of the continent. For in these royal families, who have intermarried through the centuries, flows the blood of all European nations. They are the touchstone of peoples separated by geography and time. Prince Charles of Great Britain has observed:

> There is a mystical element in royalty that one
> finds running like a thread through the his-
> tory of the world—all monarchies possess it,
> as we can see looking thousands of years into
> the past. Let us then retain this quality while,
> at the same time, perhaps associating it with a
> more modern, more contemporary image.[33]

If the European Community is the test bed for world
government, then the creation of a European monarch
could easily be "grown" to fit a global throne.

Doorstep of Two Kingdoms

Today there is a rising call for world government and
monarchy. Together the path-ways of government and
power are beginning to converge on the milestone of the
kingdom of the evil prince. These current developments
on the pathways of government and power are charac-
teristic of and consistent with the biblical description of
the prince's kingdom.

We are now in a period of transition—a key moment
for shaping events for years to come. Nation-states are
losing control and sovereignty to supranational bodies.
Rather than ushering in the Utopian, democratic reign
of peace that people so desire, the world is about to
accept the worst form of authoritarian government ever
to have emerged on the face of the planet.

For the world, these pathways are leading toward
judgment, destruction, and the doorstep of the kingdom
of the evil prince. For Messiah's bride, this moment of
transition is yet another sign that her blessed Lord and
Bridegroom is almost at the door. We are standing on the
doorstep of the kingdom of God!

4

THE
EUROPEAN
PATHWAY

The pathway of Europe is the pathway of Imperial Rome; it is a continuum. Just as Imperial Rome expanded and conquered the civilized world, Europe has continued to colonize, evangelize, industrialize, and inculturate the entire planet. Europe's hybrid language—English, Western culture, and democracy—have been globally adopted as standards. The United States, the largest European colony, has greatly assisted in the spread of "European" culture and values. Where in the world can you travel without encountering an American fast-food restaurant, an American Express office, and *The Terminator* dubbed in the local vernacular?

Characteristics of the Empire

In its early days, Europe conquered the world by military might. Today, Europe's might is economic. While the rest of the world has been financially bulimic—periodically binging and purging, thereby ruining their long-term financial health—Europe has been eating sensibly and taking steroids. Despite being temporarily out of form after German reunification, Europe has become *the* economic powerhouse, and Germany is its engine. Europe's ultimate control over the planet's economy will be no less subtle than military occupation. The world is about to face the ultimate "hostile takeover." But that takeover bid will not be launched by a corporate raider; it will be launched by the evil prince. The result of his efforts will be the creation of a European-based world empire, one that has been described in detail by God's prophets. Before we discuss how the pathway of Europe is leading us ever closer to the milestone of the kingdom of the evil prince, let's review some of the characteristics of that empire.

- ◆ It is a European empire.[1]

- ◆ It is a kingdom comprised of other kingdoms.[2]

- ◆ It is a divided kingdom, with some parts weak and others strong.[3]

- ◆ One of its subsidiary kingdoms has recently recovered from a mortal wound, perhaps a military defeat.[4]

- ◆ Its awesome strength is used to subject the whole earth.[5]

- ◆ It is different from the other kingdoms.[6]

- ◆ Prior to the evil prince's rise to power, there are ten kings.[7]

- ◆ During the reign of these ten kings, an eleventh king arises, who is different from the ten—our evil prince.[8]

   He eliminates three of the ten kings.[9]

   He wages war against God's people.[10]

He speaks out against God.[11]

He has himself deified.[12]

He will honor a god of fortifications.[13]

He honors those who acknowledge him, and gives them ruling authority.[14]

He intends to change times and law.[15]

He rules for 3½ years.[16]

He rules with a cabinet of ten men.[17]

His cabinet chief wields the prince's power as his own.[18]

His cabinet chief institutes an economic system which controls all buying and selling.[19]

♦ It is judged by God and dominion is given to Messiah.[20]

Since the world embarked on the European pathway around 264 B.C. (more than 2200 years ago), the turrets of this European fortress could be seen in the distance! With each step on the path this kingdom draws closer and can be seen more clearly. It has been a long journey. The pathway of Europe is about to lead us over the drawbridge into the realm of the evil prince.

To understand more about this kingdom, and how we will get from where we now stand on the pathway of Europe to that point, requires an understanding of Europe's overall development, for some of the characteristics of this pathway are common throughout its length. Europe has three major periods of development: unification, division, and reunification. In each of these phases the civil government has been closely tied to religion.

Evolution of the European Empire

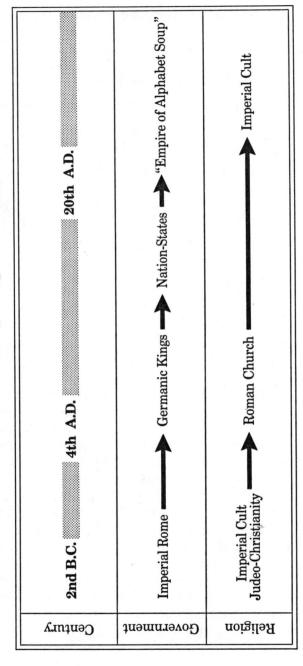

Century	2nd B.C.	4th A.D.	20th A.D.
Government	Imperial Rome	→ Germanic Kings →	Nation-States → "Empire of Alphabet Soup"
Religion	Imperial Cult Judeo-Christianity	→ Roman Church →	Imperial Cult

Unification:

- The Roman Empire was created through military conquest and inculturation.
- The world empire was centrally controlled by the city-state of Rome.
- In addition to worshiping local gods, the emperor was also worshiped.
- Judeo-Christianity could not accept emperor worship and was persecuted.
- The central government lost control due to overexpansion and eventually fell during invasions by Germanic tribes.

Division:

- Germanic tribes invaded all of Europe and Germanic kings began to rule local areas.
- The geographic influence of local kings grew and the age of the absolute monarch and nation-state was born.
- During this period, a number of attempts were made to reunify Europe, including: the Holy Roman Empire, the French Empire, the German Empire, and the Third Reich.
- The Roman Church's political influence grew and was intertwined with that of the European kings.
- Judaism and non-Roman Christianity were persecuted for not accepting the preeminence of Roman Church doctrine.

Reunification:

- The European empire will continue to expand through economic conquest and inculturation.

- Europe's government will be two-tiered, born of an "alphabet soup" of weak and strong governmental organizations—CSCE, EC, NATO, et al.

- The European empire is currently centrally controlled from Brussels, but will eventually be controlled from Jerusalem.

- In addition to worshiping local and New Age gods, the evil prince (the modern Roman emperor) will also be worshiped.

- Judeo-Christianity will not accept emperor worship and will be persecuted. In this phase, the Roman Church will find itself on the receiving end of persecution as well.

- The central government will struggle to retain global control, but will eventually fall during a war with Israel's Messiah.

Prophetic events do not just jump out of the woodwork; they are God's previews of the natural continuation of history into the future. Europe's future is integrally tied to its past. In that this path will directly lead to the kingdom of the evil prince, our understanding of its past and present is vital. So let's do an overflight of the entire European pathway.

European Unification
264 B.C. to Fourth Century A.D.

It is difficult for us to imagine how one world government will evolve out of the confusion of European organizations. We read prophecies of this government's brutal oppression of God's people and wonder why the peoples of the planet would willingly submit to this regime. Perhaps there is a clue to this mystery in the nature of Imperial Roman government and religion.

Although it is hard to believe, Imperial Rome was characterized by political and religious tolerance. It was the usual practice of conquering nations to enslave the local populations and force them to accept their appointed governors and alien religion. Not so with Rome.

The Romans were a practical people; their objective was to collect taxes. Oppressed people are uncooperative, and uncooperative people do not pay taxes. Therefore Rome conquered through cultural assimilation. The Romans built a vast network of roads throughout their empire. Although the primary intent was for the movement of troops, these roads also served as a conduit for Roman civilization. The Romans taught provincial civil servants and magistrates the Roman method of government, then let them rule their own people.

The Romans themselves imported the "best" features of local cultures and religions and integrated them into the whole of Roman civilization. Rome was therefore the sum of its parts. Each race and religion was able to find suitable breathing room in this early "common European house," with the notable exception of the Jews.

So extensive was this "unity in diversity," a concept that we hear so much of in our day, that by the first century A.D. few members of the Roman Senate were of Italian extraction. Rome was not always viewed as an occupying force, since the Romans were often more efficient and benevolent than the local governments that they replaced. Provincial peoples treasured their Roman citizenship because of the security and legal benefits it bestowed. We have an example of this in Acts 22, where the apostle Paul struck terror into the hearts of his Roman captors when he informed them of his Roman citizenship.

Roman religion was very eclectic. It was a massive collection of amorphous beliefs and tribal gods. There was no defined creed of dogma. The gods of conquered nations were quickly assimilated into the whole.

The Romans viewed religion much differently than we who live in a society rooted in the Judeo-Christian tradition. Religion was not thought of in terms of salvation or individual behavior. Rather, "religion" was the performance of required public rites by the local magistrates. To the very practical common man, religion meant little more than not working on the holidays. But as with most "practical" people of any era, when they sought the meaning of life, they turned to superstitions and crazes. During this period there was a great influx of religious ideas and practices from the East.

Amidst this potpourri of beliefs arose an Imperial cult. In 12 B.C. Augustus Caesar, ruler of Imperial Rome, assumed the role of chief priest of the official cult and its title of Pontifex Maximus. (This is the same title currently held by the Roman Catholic Pope, the Bishop of Rome.) Augustus used the position to revive the old Roman religious ideas. These included linking respect for patrons, placating and invoking deities, and commemorating great events and men to divine kingship. In the provinces he allowed worship of his genius: a divine life-force within him. Most provincial religions did not find the Imperial cult restrictive. After all, what is another god among hundreds of others? The exception to this were the Jews. Although not happy with their loss of sovereignty, they could reconcile themselves to paying taxes. What they could not tolerate was the blasphemy of worshiping a Roman emperor as a god. This friction continued until open revolt broke out in 66 A.D., which ultimately resulted in the destruction of the second temple in 70 A.D.

Today we see these same trends toward European unity through cultural assimilation and religious "tolerance." Through worldwide electronic communications, English has become the world's common language;

Western civilization and Western democracy have become the world's leading form of government; and "religion" has become whatever a person wants it to be. Just as in the days of ancient Rome, the world has been totally "Romanized." We are well along the road to world citizenship.

European Division
Fourth Century A.D.
to Mid-Twentieth Century

After seven centuries of unification, European central government fell. The reasons for the fall of Rome literally fill volumes. For our discussion it is important to note that the German people have played a key role in the division and subsequent reunification of Europe. The central government of Rome collapsed during invasions and migrations by Germanic tribes. These tribes established Germanic kingdoms throughout Europe.

Major Germanic Conquests and Migrations

Area	Germanic Tribes
Britain	Angles and Saxons
Spain	Visigoths
Italy	Ostrogoths and Lombards
Gaul	Franks, Burgundians, Visigoths
North Africa	Vandals

German blood and culture was intermixed throughout the continent of Europe. Today, are not the British referred to by the Germanic tribal name "Anglo-Saxons"? Have you heard of European Gothic architecture, coined to indicate its barbarism? Are the people from Roman Gaul not now called the "French," from the Germanic tribe of the "Franks"? Does not Burgundy wine come from that area settled by the Germanic Burgundians in France? It is also interesting to note that most, if not all, of the European monarchies have Germanic roots.

Despite this common heritage, for 1600 years Europe has been plagued with warfare and division. Perhaps this is what the prophet Daniel was alluding to when he said:

> In that you saw the iron mixed with common clay, they will combine with one another in the seed of men; but they will not adhere to one another, even as iron does not combine with pottery (Daniel 2:43).

The Germanic tribes established kingdoms and "feudal" domains throughout Europe. As the geographic influence of the local kings grew, the age of the absolute monarch and nation-state was born. During this period, successive attempts were made to centrally govern and reunify Europe. Since the fall of Imperial Rome, these reunification attempts almost appear as a single, organized, unbroken effort to reestablish a unified Europe. Considering that when true reunification does take place, the unified Europe will have world dominion, the appellation of a "satanic plot" may not be totally out of order.

The Frankish Kingdom (482-814)

King Clovis defeated the Roman armies in Gaul (modern France). He was king of the Franks, a Germanic warrior tribe. His successors expanded his kingdom so that it encompassed nearly the whole of Europe. They "...not only extended Frankish overlordship in the east as far as the middle Danube, but also conquered the Burgundians and drove the Ostrogoths from Provence."[21] However, Clovis' heirs were known as "do-nothing" kings. It was during their reigns that the power of the nobility grew.

A powerful lineage of nobles, the Mayors of the Palace, succeeded to the Frankish throne in 751 with the help of the Pope. In exchange, King Pepin defeated the Germanic Lombards of Northern Italy and gave the land to the Pope. Pepin's son was Charlemagne. After conquering the Lombards in Italy, the Moslems in Spain, the Slavs in Czechoslovakia, and the Saxons in northwest Germany, Charlemagne was rewarded by the Roman Church. In 800 he was crowned "Emperor of the Romans" by Pope Leo II. Charlemagne's empire collapsed upon his death in 814 and his title was unused until 962.

The Holy Roman Empire (962-1806)

The Holy Roman Empire "... was effectively established in 962 when the pope crowned Otto I, king of Germany, emperor at Rome. At its height in the 10th and 11th centuries, it included all the German lands, Austria, and modern West Czechoslovakia, Switzerland, the Low Countries, Eastern France and Northern and Central Italy. The emperor was usually the dominant German sovereign, elected by the princes and until Maximilian I, crowned by the pope. The empire was originally seen as a universal monarchy, modeled on the Roman Empire, the temporal equivalent and ally of the papacy. From the 11th to the 13th centuries, however, it clashed continually with the papacy for European supremacy.... The empire endured in name until Napoleon, as Emperor of the French, ceased to recognize it in 1806; Francis II of Austria then abdicated the imperial title."[22]

Perhaps this model of a European head of state being elected by his peers and crowned by the Pope will be the model by which the evil prince will ascend to his throne!

The French Empire (1804-1815)

In 1804 Napoleon changed France's government from a republic into an empire. He assumed the title of Emperor Napoleon I. With the exception of Portugal and Britain, Napoleon's empire dominated the continent of Europe from the Atlantic Ocean to the Russian border. The rise of Napoleon was the demise of the Holy Roman Empire.

In addition to military conquest, Napoleon engaged in economic warfare as well. He isolated Britain from continental markets by developing the "Continental System" and sought to overtake her colonial possessions as well. Initially Russia, who was allied with Napoleon, agreed to boycott English markets. However, after suffering economically, Russia resumed a trading relationship with Britain. Napoleon then attacked Russia but was forced to retreat. This began the decline of Napoleon's empire, which ended at Waterloo. After the fall of Napoleon's empire, the rule of Europe by absolute monarchy was restored by the Congress of Vienna.

In that the evil prince's primary area of control will be economic, perhaps it will be the fear of exclusion from a neo-continental system that will cause nations to rush to join his empire.

The German Empire (1789-1945)

The road to German unity has been a long one. Prior to the domination of Europe by Napoleon there were over 300 German states. Through consolidation, Napoleon reduced that number to 100. The Congress of Vienna, which attempted to patch Europe back together after the Napoleonic disaster, further reduced the number of Germanic states to 38.

Between 1862 and 1871, Prussia, one of the larger Germanic states, sought to unify Germans and create a single state. Otto von Bismark sought to expedite unification by giving the Germans a common foe. He intentionally provoked the Franco-Prussian War. This war began a period of hostilities that would eventually precipitate two world wars. In 1871 his scheming paid off and the German Empire was born. William I was proclaimed Kaiser (Caesar). This empire initially stretched through much of north-central Europe and Russia.

The northern Germanic states were predominantly Protestant, while the south was predominantly Catholic. After the German Empire was created, Bismark began a legislative attack against the Roman Church called "Kulturkampf"—"struggle for civilization." The Roman clergy was placed under state control. The Church could no longer influence education. All marriages had to be civil ceremonies. This renewed the tradition of religious persecution in Europe. After many years of hatred and military buildup, the Franco-Prussian war again erupted, this time as World War I. Then, on the pretext of defending German ethnic nationals, Germany and its allies conquered much of the continent of Europe during the 1930's. This was Adolph Hitler's Third Reich and the beginning of World War II.

During this dark period, religious hatred again flared. The Nazis controlled the Protestant churches. Those churchmen who would not cooperate were placed in concentration camps. The Roman clergy was often framed and incarcerated. Catholic education was discouraged. The Nazi regime had a particular hatred for the Jews. German Jews were deprived of citizenship, their synagogues were burned, their property was confiscated, their means of livelihood was removed, and they were transported to concentration camps, where they were systematically starved, tortured, and murdered. German domination of Europe and the carnage of God's people was stopped when Germany was defeated by Russian, British, and U.S. forces.

Perhaps the German Empire will be the model for the evil prince's religious persecution. He too will take great delight in oppressing the Jews and occupying their rebuilt temple in Jerusalem. He and his cabinet of ten will also take great delight in burning Vatican City.[23]

Since the breakup of Rome, there have been continuous efforts to "put it back together again," as the Humpty-Dumpty rhyme goes. It would appear that God has stayed the hand of the unifiers for two millennia so that He could implement His own plan of grace. Today the unifiers are having increasing success. One Nazi legacy was the seed of the current reunification effort—the European Coal and Steel Community. But more on that later. Soon a "Roman"-based world government will be in place, with the evil prince wearing its crown. He will have studied his European history well, and learned its lessons of kingship, economic dominion, and religious persecution.

The Role of the Roman Church

Just as the Imperial Cult was intertwined with Imperial Rome, so the Roman Church has been intertwined with the European kings. This intermingling of the Roman Church and European government began in 313 A.D., when the Roman Emperor Constantine officially accepted "Christianity" and ended its persecution. As Emperor of Rome, Constantine was the Pontifex Maximus—leader of the Imperial Cult. That cult had its roots in the Babylonian religion. In addition to worshiping the emperor himself, it principally worshiped the mother goddess Venus and her infant son Jupiter.

The Babylonian religion is, in fact, the root of many ancient religions.[24]

Universal Scope of Mother Goddess Worship

People	Mother Goddess (and child)
Babylon	Semiramis and Tammuz
China	Shingmoo ("Holy Mother") with Child
Germany	The virgin Hertha with Child
Scandinavia	Disa with Child
Etruscans	Nutria
Druids	Virgo-Patritura
India	Indrani with Child Devaki and Crishna Isi ("The Great Goddess") and Iswara
Greece	Aphrodite
Ephesus	Diana
Egypt	Isis and Horus
Sumeria	Nana
Asia	Cybele and Deoius
Canaan	Ashtaroth ("The Queen of Heaven")
Rome	Venus and Jupiter

Note: It is also interesting to note that some of these goddesses (Semiramis and Diana, for example) are considered "goddesses of fortifications." In Daniel 11:38 we are told that the evil prince will honor a deity of fortresses.

The adoption of Christianity by "Pontifex Maximus" Constantine led to the inevitable intermingling of Babylonian and Christian religious traditions. It was not long before a faithful Jewish woman named Miriam was worshiped as the mother goddess "Mary" and her messianic Son, Yeshua, was pictured as the "baby Jesus" in her arms. To the average citizen of Rome, the change in the state religion was transparent.

Thus began the Roman Church's accelerated departure from its Judaic, apostolic roots. In his dual role as head of the Roman government and the Roman Church, Constantine himself presided over the Council of Nicaea. This council hammered out the doctrinal positions of the church and developed the Nicene Creed.

Another major development in relations between the Roman Church and European government occurred with the crownings of Charlemagne as "Emperor of the Romans" and Otto I as Emperor of the Holy Roman Empire. By these papal coronations of civil rulers, the Roman Church claimed the right to enthrone and dethrone kings and emperors.

The Roman Church became a form of supranational government. In that most of the people of Europe were Catholic, they were spiritually governed by the Roman Church, and civilly governed by kings and emperors who ruled at the discretion of the Roman Church. When kings had disputes with the Roman Church, they also had to deal with the backlash from their Catholic subjects. In Revelation 17 John describes a woman, "mystery Babylon," riding a scarlet beast. He tells us that the woman is a religious organization and the beast is a collection of kings. Perhaps it is this control over the European kings that the Roman Church has had in the past and may yet have in the future that the apostle John had in mind in the book of Revelation.

European Reunification
Mid-Twentieth Century to the Future

There is a lot of ground to cover in discussing the reunification efforts of the postwar period. In this section we will cover:

* The major "alphabet soup" organizations that constitute the new Europe.

* The unusual method in which nations select their level of commitment to the new Europe.

* 1990 as a landmark year in the rebirth of the three major organizations of Europe: NATO, the CSCE, and the EC.

* The expansion of Europe through treaties with nonmembers.

* The power centers of European government.

* The role of religion in the reunified Europe.

This section of the pathway of Europe may soon lead to the milestones of the Middle East Peace Covenant, the kingdom of the evil prince, and Armageddon.

European Alphabet Soup

The heart of the new European empire is economic. That heart has been developing since the fall of the German Empire in the 1940's, thus continuing the historic movement toward reunification. The "granddaddy" of all European organizations is the ECSC, the European Coal and Steel Community, founded in 1951.

In 1943 Monnet [the "Father of Europe"] drafted a note de reflexion about the peace that should follow victory over Hitler's Germany. This, he thought, could only be achieved through an entirely new organization embracing the European nations and their economies. This note contained many aspects of the proposals he was to submit in 1950 to the then French Foreign Minister, Robert Schuman. These proposals, known as the Schuman Plan, gave birth to the first of the European Communities, the European Coal and Steel Community, which pooled the iron, steel and coal industries of France, Germany, Italy and the Benelux [Belgium, the Netherlands, Luxembourg] countries (soon to be known as the Six) under the first supranational body, the High Authority—forerunner of the European Commission. The other five nations had the common experience of German occupation and control over their industry. Since the German industrial complex had been centrally directed to the war effort, there had been considerable cooperation between all six nations, especially in resistance to the demands which were being made on them by Albert Speer, the Nazi industrial supremo. Grounded in part, therefore, on their recent experience, the coal and steel industries of the continent were a natural first step for formal collaboration. The founding treaty of this first Community was signed in Paris on 18 April 1951.[25]

Since the creation of the ECSC, Europe has been coalescing and pressing on toward the goal of creating a single, borderless European market. The current European market of 340 million people is the "flame" that is attracting other nations to that union. But a government cannot deal solely with economic issues. In order to be functional, a centralized European government will have to be balanced and provide a complete portfolio of federal services.

The government of Europe at this stage of development is an "alphabet soup" of organizations and agencies. It is very easy to get lost in all the acronyms. In order to become a cohesive union, Europe is undergoing a "rationalization" process. That is to say, the organizations which functionally overlap will either be combined or weeded out, leaving a single, strong, multifunctional government.

In the following chart you will see some of the primary organizations that have been operating in both East and West Europe.

Europe, Cafeteria-Style

At least for the short term, the new Europe is going to be "cafeteria style." That is to say, a nation joining the new Europe will be able to pick and choose its level of commitment. J. Walker reported in the *International Herald Tribune*:

> In the near term, European security arrangements will be more patchwork than architecture—a series of partial, overlapping and changing arrangements building on the European Community, NATO and CSCE. This may offend tidy minds, but its very flexibility will be more suited to a changing Europe than anyone's grand design.

The current level of participation of various nations in what could collectively be called the "new Europe" varies greatly. Some nations participate marginally, while others have "sold the ranch" in order to participate at the deepest levels.

At the very heart of the new Europe is Germany, which keeps occupying center stage in the development of Europe. It was the Germanic tribes that destroyed

Summary: European Alphabet Soup

Economic		
EC	European Community (used interchangeably with the European Economic Community)	◆ Objective: Establishment of a common market where people, goods, and services can move freely across the borders of member states. ◆ 12 West European nations.
EFTA	European Free Trade Association	◆ Objective: A free trade association of six nations with limited demands on national sovereignty. ◆ Launched by Britain as an alternative to the European Community; Britain subsequently "jumped ship" and joined the EC.
EEA	European Economic Area	◆ Objective: To establish a trading relation between the EFTA and the EC and to serve as an anteroom for new EC aspirants. ◆ Formal agreement agreed on in 1991. Still being clarified in early 1992.
COMECON		◆ Objective: Trading bloc of Communist nations during their heyday. ◆ Six East European nations plus the USSR, Cuba, Mongolia, and Vietnam.

Military		
NATO	North Atlantic Treaty Organization	◆ Objective: Originally, to defend the West against Soviet aggression; seeking a new vision in the post-Soviet world. ◆ 14 West European Nations plus U.S. and Canada. (Russia has applied for membership.)
WARSAW PACT	Warsaw Treaty Organization	◆ Objective: Defend the East against West European aggression. ◆ Seven East European nations plus the USSR. ◆ "Went out of business" on March 31, 1991.
Security and Defense		
CSCE	Conference on Security and Cooperation in Europe	◆ Objective: International problem resolution; similar to U.N. but limited to first-and second-world nations. ◆ 34 nations: All of Europe (excluding Albania), the U.S., and Canada. ◆ Strategic level negotiations. ◆ Doorway for U.S., Canada, and USSR into the new Europe.
WEU	Western European Union	◆ Objective: Coordination of defense policies for major European nations. ◆ Originally created to oversee German rearmament during the Cold War. ◆ May become the coordinated voice of a federal Europe in NATO.

Imperial Rome. It was these same Germanic tribes who migrated throughout Europe and "combined with one another in the seed of men."[26] It has been the Germans and the Germanic "Franks" who have been behind most if not all European reunification efforts. According to *U.S. News:*

> People don't realize how dominant an economic power the Germans are. They are a bigger trading nation than Japan, and they will become even more powerful because they will be the focal point of a European economic boom during the 1990's. That's because many German institutions—principally the Bundesbank, the country's central bank—will be the center of economic gravity.[27]

I expect that the recent economic setbacks which Germany has experienced as a result of reunification and the Gulf War will be temporary. However, one of the immediate benefits of Germany's economic downturn has been a reduction in European fear of an Imperial Germany ruling a united Europe. Germany now appears much less daunting and much more vulnerable. The reduction of suspicions and fears will serve to speed European integration.

There is also a third dimension to this unification phenomenon: The nations vary in their level of commitment to the federalist aspirations of these organizations. For example, both Britain and Germany are members of the EC, but sovereign Britain is riding the brakes while federalist Germany is attempting to open the throttle.

In most European organizations, nations can be affiliated either strongly or weakly, depending upon their own sensibilities. Daniel writes in his second chapter that the parts of the evil prince's kingdom will be composed of "iron and clay"—that is, some will be strong and some will be weak. He also said that this coming kingdom would be "different" from others. Perhaps this is Daniel's way of describing this unusual, patchwork alliance of nations.

1990 and the Rebirth of Europe

The year 1990 marked the beginning of European reconstruction. Time permitting, this reconstruction will continue throughout the decade. The restructuring process has so far included the North Atlantic Treaty Organization (NATO), the Conference on Security and Cooperation in Europe (CSCE), and the European Community (EC). Together these three organizations form the core of the new Europe.

The New NATO

The restructuring of NATO and the CSCE began in July of 1990 at the NATO Summit in London. American President George Bush characterized the Summit as a "historic turning point" that charts "a new path for peace." He further stated, "For more than 40 years we've looked for this day. And now that day is here, and all peoples from the Atlantic to the Urals, from the Baltic to the Adriatic, can share in its promise." Soviet Foreign Minister Shevardnadze said of the Final Declaration that was issued at the conclusion of the Summit, "This creates a fundamentally different political climate in Europe and, given its consistent implementation in life, may form a conceptual foundation for a new security system in the continent." The *New York Times* of July 7, 1990, stated, "...history was in the air here, a sense of a new Europe, a place whose 'future belongs to freedom, partnership and openness' in the hopeful words of Manfred Worner, the NATO Secretary General."

The reason for these hopeful if not jubilant expressions was the "visionary" text of the Final Declaration, which began:

> Europe has entered a new, promising era. Central and Eastern Europe is liberating itself. The Soviet Union has embarked on the long journey toward a free society. The walls that once confined people and ideas are collapsing. Europeans are determining their own destiny. They are choosing freedom. They are choosing economic liberty. They are choosing peace. They are choosing a Europe whole and free. As a consequence, this Alliance must and will adapt.... We recognize that, in the new Europe, the security of every state is inseparably linked to the security of its neighbors. NATO must become an institution where Europeans, Canadians and Americans work together not only for the common defense, but to build new partnerships with all the nations of Europe.

The declaration outlined concrete actions that will transform NATO from "the most successful defensive alliance in history" into "an agent for change... build-[ing] the structures of a more united continent, supporting security and stability with the strength of our shared faith in democracy, the rights of the individual, and the peaceful resolution of disputes." It included a joint statement of non-agression with the Warsaw Pact and laid out a new blueprint for the CSCE.

The Final Declaration concluded by saying:

Today, our Alliance begins a major transformation. Working with all the countries of Europe, we are determined to create enduring peace on this continent.

NATO is indeed undergoing a transformation. It is attempting to downplay its military role at the moment and formulate a new political role. The Declaration addressed NATO's new short-and-long-term goals as a "political" institution. By immediately extending a hand to the Soviets and the Eastern Bloc, it assuaged Soviet opposition to German reunification and incorporation into the NATO Alliance, and hastened the dissolution of the Warsaw Pact. That pact was formally dissolved on March 31, 1991.

More importantly, NATO seemed to be pointing to the day when it would become a companion of the CSCE in forming the new European government. The summit addressed at great length a new blueprint for the CSCE.

The New CSCE

The Conference on Security and Cooperation in Europe is the "United Nations" of Europe. Unlike the original U.N., it is an organization that was bought and paid for by Europe and is immune to the meddling of third-world nations. The CSCE may be the foundation on which Europe can construct its economic fortress and cause every nation to fall under its influence.

Until 1990 the CSCE was an itinerant "sewing circle" of nations which came together for a spot of tea and to chat about human rights. In 1990 that changed!

On November 21, 1990, shortly after the historic NATO Summit, the 34 nations of the Conference on Security and Cooperation in Europe (CSCE) signed the "Charter of Paris for a New Europe." The Charter was described as a Magna Charta or Bill of Rights. Reports in the media were generally dismissive. When most analysts looked at the charter, they saw touchy-feely language with little substance. But make no mistake, this treaty is the foundation stone for the much-heralded "New World Order" centered in Europe. That final world order which is coming into view is not the recent vision of George Bush, but the vision of God's prophets.

The "Charter of Paris for a New Europe" established "democracy as the only system of government" for its signatories. It also formalized a universal set of freedoms and rights. It is upon those freedoms and rights that the CSCE membership plans "to construct the new Europe." The Charter specifically cites the following:

Freedom of:	thought, conscience, and religion; expression; association and peaceful assembly; movement.
Freedom from:	arbitrary arrest or detention; torture or other cruel, inhuman, or degrading treatment or punishment.
Rights:	to know and act upon rights; to participate in free and fair elections; to fair and public trial if charged with an offense; to own property; to exercise individual enterprise; to enjoy economic, social, and cultural rights; to affirm the protection of ethnic, cultural, linguistic, and religious identity of national minorities.

On face value, it appeared that the treaty's only objective was to declare an end to the Cold War and to inaugurate the "new European era." The charter begins:

We, the heads of state or government of the states participating in the Conference on Security and Cooperation in Europe, have assembled in Paris at a time of profound change and historic expectations. The era of confrontation and division of Europe has ended. We declare that henceforth our relations will be founded on respect and cooperation.

The treaty is a strategic plan. In fact, the Soviet Union and Eastern bloc nations had been hoping for a more "operational" agreement that would transform the CSCE into a pan-European security agency, now that the Warsaw Pact was clinically dead. Their hopes were not realized.

However, the "Charter of Paris for a New Europe" did nothing less than codify European civilization. It has institutionalized a common value system for Europe and North America. As the Charter itself states, it is the intent of the signatories "to construct the new Europe" upon those common precepts. And build they will. In fact the building has already begun. In addition to establishing a "secretariat" or bureaucracy for the CSCE, the Charter has also laid the groundwork for building a two-tiered European government, and has called all nations to join the CSCE in protecting the "community of fundamental human values."

In this building process it is easier to organize similar things than grossly dissimilar things. The "Charter of Paris for a New Europe" has laid a common foundation among European peoples. This commonality of values, laws, and institutions will make the job of creating a cogent, supranational, European government much easier. Most ideological barriers have been transcended. Now the task is to build governmental bodies and agencies which will support those values.

Again, we can see that this new European Empire is strikingly similar to the kingdom of the evil prince described in the Bible. CSCE architects are building a European government with worldwide influence, paying special attention to the "ethnic, cultural, linguistic and religious identity of national minorities."

This is similar to the authority given to the evil prince. He is given "authority over every tribe and people and tongue and nation" (Revelation 13:7)...or "national minorities," to use the modern terminology.

It is safe to say that the European collage under construction will be "different from all other kingdoms." And it already encompasses much of the earth. Perhaps this is what Daniel had in mind when he wrote that this last empire "will be different from all other kingdoms, and it will devour the whole earth and tread it down and crush it" (Daniel 7:23).

With the signing of the "Charter of Paris for a New Europe" the foundation for the kingdom of the evil prince is now in place and serious construction is underway.

The New EC

According to authors Buchan and Colchester:

> Economics is, au fond, the driving force behind politics in the modern world. There is much greater awareness today of the way that the political and military fortunes of states, empires, and coalitions have through the centuries undulated up and down according to their relative economic positions. The most striking late-20th-century examples of this truth are Japan, with riches and no rockets, and the Soviet Union, with rockets and no riches.[28]

It is no accident that the Europeans are making the heart of their new empire an exclusive economic club— the European Community. Economic might is power. There has been great international concern that Europe could use that power to construct a protective economic fortress. Community outsiders have worried about being locked out of "Fortress Europe," a term originally coined by Nazi Propaganda Minister Joseph Goebels.[29] For those who have studied the economic privation suffered by Britain when locked out of Napoleon's Continental System, this is no idle threat. This fear of exclusion, and the reactionary rush for inclusion, have radically increased the flow of EC membership aspirants. In order to handle this influx, the EC is being restructured.

Like the 13 American colonies, the nations of Europe are struggling to define their growing relationship. The American colonies needed a body to govern their joint affairs. As a result of this need, in 1781 the Articles of Confederation, which loosely bound the post-Revolution American colonies together, came into effect. By 1787 the "states" had outgrown that treaty. So for four months of that year, delegates from each state met together in Philadelphia for a constitutional convention. From that convention emerged the U.S. Constitution, which has framed the form of the U.S. federal government and its relations to the member states for over 200 years.

This path of constitutional reform is currently being walked by the European Community. In 1957 the founding Treaty of Rome was enacted. It loosely bound the economic policies of the European Community's member nations and made room for national sovereignty. In the mid 1980's the European Community established "Project 1992." Its objective was to pass at least 280 measures that would create a single, borderless European market by December 31, 1992. It soon became clear that the provisions of the Treaty of Rome were inhibiting passage of the required measures.

Therefore in 1986 the Single European Act (SEA) was signed. This "single" act was actually pork barrel legislation which provided one or more Treaty amendments to make each member state happy. The SEA "greased the wheels" of the EC. By providing for a broader use of majority voting, issues which had been held up waiting for unanimity were rapidly passed. The work yet ahead is daunting. Currently the European Community is feverishly trying to meet its 1992 deadline.

Issues which arose in the late 1980's caused the EC to further reexamine its structure. Internally, federalists began to envision the EC's purview expanded to include the areas of foreign policy, monetary, and defense policies. Externally, the revolutions in Eastern Europe and the threat of being locked out of "Fortress Europe" caused membership inquiries to flood in.

By 1990 the member nations of the European Community had outgrown the founding Treaty of Rome. Without major changes to that treaty, they could not deepen their internal unity to include other governmental issues, nor could the structure of the Community handle a great influx of new members if the Community was externally widened. In December 1990 a European brand of "constitutional conventions" began, which are poetically called "Intergovernmental Conferences." One conference is addressing political union and restructuring of the EC government, while the other is addressing economic and monetary union.

The Conference on Political Union

Currently the political affairs of Europe are handled by the European Political Cooperation Council (EPC), an organization that consists of 12 national foreign ministries. In the past the EPC's powers have been severely limited by contention among the member nations and unanimous voting requirements that kill most efforts toward joint action. Replacing the EPC with a viable foreign policy mechanism is one of the chief issues being addressed by the conference on political union.

The weakness of the EPC was recently highlighted by the Gulf War. Just before the war began, Belgian foreign minister Mark Eyskens observed:

Europe is an economic giant, a political dwarf, and a military worm.[30]

There was no "Europe" when it came to Gulf War activities. Certainly European nations participated individually, but their response was far from unified. Many journalists pointed to this disunity as proof positive that there will never be a unified Europe.

But just the opposite may be true. The absence of "Europe" on the world political stage at that defining moment is being used by European federalists to embarrass the EC membership into accepting stronger union.

As a result of the work of the Intergovernmental Conference on Political Union, we could see—

* the kingdom of the evil prince being rapidly built, perhaps on the foundation laid by the "Charter of Paris for a New Europe";

* the pathway of Europe approaching the milestone of the Middle East Peace Convenant.

The Conference on Economic and Monetary Union

Some of the primary objectives of the Intergovernmental Conference on Economic and Monetary Union (EMU) are the development of a common currency and creation of a central bank to manage it. This is essential for a "borderless market." Can you imagine the economic nightmare if the U.S. had 50 different state currencies?

Federalists in Europe are hoping to realize huge cost savings and increased global influence by having a single, common currency. Recent debate has centered on this issue: When introducing that common currency, should it be as a replacement for national currencies, or as a parallel, thirteenth currency? A common currency will have to be managed; therefore a central bank or "Eurofed" is being proposed. Just as the Federal Reserve controls the availability of currency and interest rates for the U.S., so a European central bank will control European currency availability and interest rates. Some member nations are resisting this encroachment on national economic sovereignty. This is a bitter pill to swallow for some, particularly the British.

The need for a central bank became obvious in December 1978, when the European Monetary System (EMS) was born. The purpose of this system was to stabilize European monetary exchange rates by tying member currencies to the European Currency Unit (ECU), which is roughly a weighted average of member currencies. By keeping their exchange rates within a prescribed variance from the ECU, member nations have been coordinating their economies and rates of inflation.

The European Monetary System did not, however, establish a central bank to provide central coordination of currencies. This vacuum has been filled by the German central bank.

> Most of Europe has been turned into a Deutschmark zone. The Bundesbank in Frankfurt has become Europe's de facto central bank. Other EMS participants have to ape a German monetary policy in which they have no formal say. If they are lucky, they will get advance warnings from the Bundesbank that it is about to raise or lower its interest rates.[31]

Therefore, failure of the Conference on Economic and Monetary Union to achieve agreement on the creation of a common currency and central bank will mean continued domination of Europe by the German central bankers. On the other hand, the successful construction of a European currency and central bank would crystallize the power of Europe. "The role of the reserve bank would be crucial; the effect of such a dirigiste institution would be incalculable but far-reaching. It represents a major step forward, one that not all may prove willing to take."[32]

When the final structure of the new Europe is proposed, some European Community members may not be able to control their budgets, or more importantly, be willing to sacrifice their national sovereignty. In Daniel 7:24 we are told of ten kings, three of whom are subdued when the evil prince rises to power. Perhaps this represents the weeding out of the fainthearted from the core of the new Europe.

Britain has been a key candidate for this weeding out. In the days of Napoleon and Hitler, while Europe was under central, dictatorial control, Britain stood alone offshore. It was through the efforts of Britain and her allies that continental Europe was repeatedly liberated. These experiences have made the British very skeptical of strong Continental government. In recent years, Margaret Thatcher led Britain in actively resisting European federalism. Then the federalists orchestrated her fall from power. Today, Britain's Prime Minister Major is walking a thin line. He very much wants Britain to be inside "Fortress Europe" when the drawbridge is raised, but he is also having difficulty selling out British sovereignty. We will have to watch and see if Britain makes the "cut" to be at the core of the new Europe.

As some leaders hesitate the surrender of their nations' sovereignty, others are trying to expand the European model with religious fervor. Just as the political model for a new Europe could be used to create a world government, the currency model could be used as a model for a world currency. The vision for a unified currency is not limited to Europe. On January 9, 1988, *The Economist* made the uncharacteristically rash prediction that a world currency was in the making. They creatively called it "the phoenix," in that it would arise from the ashes of other world currencies. They cautiously predicted that the phoenix would make its appearance around the year 2018.

The Prince's Cabinet Chief

In Revelation 13 we are introduced to the evil prince's "cabinet chief" or false prophet. Among many other activities, this cabinet chief (v. 12) implements a centralized, worldwide financial system. This system provides centralized control over buying and selling (v. 17). The seeds of a common European currency and central bank currently being nurtured in the intergovernmental "hot house" may sprout into the economic system by which the evil "prince" will control the world market.

This mutant monetary system could spread like chicken pox in a nursery school. The editorial in *The Economist* provides us with a glimpse of this anticipated pandemic:

> Once Europe has a single currency in a single economic space, its system can be copied and extended. The desirable end to that process will be a world currency, serving a world economy in which trade and investment will be far more international than they are today. To clinch its attractiveness, the world currency will have to retain its purchasing power more successfully than any of the national or regional currencies it replaces. For that, it must be managed by an independent central bank which is charged with keeping the currency

stable against the price of a basket of commodities. . . .

Fanciful? It gets less so every day. Each bout of overshooting [a series of violent swings in exchange rates] brings more pain: each intervention by central banks provides less relief; each episode raises sharper questions. That pattern will not go on forever. A world currency cometh.[33]

The rise and spread of the evil prince's kingdom, in this day, at this time? Fanciful? It gets less so every day.

Expansion of the New Europe

The Treaty of Rome institutionalized a bureaucracy scaled to deal with the economic issues of a small body of nations. Since 1957, the European Community has begun to emerge as the leading economic world power of the twenty-first century. Eastern Europe, the members of the European Free Trade Association (EFTA), and other European and non-European nations are seriously evaluating their relationship with the EC. Some nations have already applied for membership. They all want to be on the winning team. In the interim, the EC has been negotiating commitments of closer relations with the United States, the EFTA, Israel, and North Africa.

At the CSCE charter summit, the United States and the EC signed the "Transatlantic Declaration on EC-US Relations." This declaration has been described as "a 'love letter' pledging closer cooperation between the European Community and the United States . . . drawn up to establish the framework for cooperation—'rooted in common values,' according to a US official—[that] would become more important as the Community's embryonic foreign policy and security role develops."[34]

The United States is also providing what may be called "secondary" expansion of Europe by creating subsidiary free trade zones with the Americas. In June of 1990, President Bush proposed a hemispheric free trade zone that would stretch from Point Barrow to Tierra del Fuego—effectively the whole of North, South, and Central America.

The EFTA currently includes Austria, Iceland, Finland, Norway, Sweden, and Switzerland. It was originally created 30 years ago as an alternative to the EC for nations which did not want to participate in a supranational state, and which did not want to surrender their legislative control. Now they fearfully stand outside the walls of "Fortress Europe." The EFTA has been negotiating a new treaty with the EC that would create a European Economic Area and allow non-EC nations to participate at a reduced level of commitment.

The agreements being entered into with the United State and the EFTA are only the beginning of Europe's expansion, which will eventually cover the earth as prophesied in Daniel 7:23. However, it looks as though the next major area of expansion is the Mediterranean Rim.

Europe and the Middle East

As we discussed earlier one of the major geopolitical milestones is the Middle East Peace Covenant. This will be a covenant that is drafted by the evil prince, is entered into by many nations, and addresses Israel's security. In the wake of the Gulf War there has been a renewed effort to achieve just such an agreement, and Europe has been attempting to play a key role in it. In recent years the bonds between the European Community and Israel have been tightening. This is not to say they have been amicable, just tighter. The EC is Israel's largest trading partner and a major creditor. The Europeans have frequently used this trading relationship to attempt to control Israel. In June 1990 the European Parliament levied sanctions against Israel[35] for its treatment of its Palestinian population and tried to force them to comply with the European Community's visions for Middle East peace.

European sympathies have always been with the Arabs. Their Arabist history has prevented them from dealing equitably with Israel. These sympathies date back to the end of World War I, when the Europeans became custodians of Arab lands formerly held by the Turkish Ottoman Empire. Since that time Europe has been fascinated with the "Bedouin mystique." This romance has impeached their judgment in the area of Arab-Israeli affairs, as evidenced by their previous betrayals of Israel.

> Western Europe now wants to play the role of mediator, "as important as that of the U.S.," in the Middle East. But its policies over the past two decades hardly provide the credentials of an honest broker. During the war of 1973, when it was clear that the Egyptian-Syrian assault placed Israel's very existence in jeopardy, West European countries, formally committed to Israel's security, refused not only to aid this country but even to grant landing rights to the American airlift.[36]

However, the Gulf War caused Europe to reevaluate their unequivocal support of the PLO. Arafat's backing of Saddam Hussein impeached the credibility of the PLO throughout the West. As a result of this rethinking, the European Parliament rescinded its sanctions against Israel. However, this does not mean that European strong-arm tactics will not continue to be used.

> In Brussels the European Community is trying to demonstrate a unity of purpose which

eluded it during the run-up to war and is moving fast to try to exercise real influence in the aftermath of conflict. Foreign ministers of the twelve meet on Monday but so far their statements on the shape of the postwar Middle East are long on hope and short on concrete proposals. It appears, however, that the Community hopes to exert itself through economic muscle.[37]

The Europeans are very anxiously pursuing an expanded role in the Middle East. In the flurry of shuttle diplomacy which followed the Gulf War, the European Community foreign ministers frequently made their position clear to American Secretary of State James Baker:

During their meeting and dinner with Mr. Baker, the ministers asked him to persuade Israel to agree to a European Community role in any international peace conference on the Middle East. Israeli officials fear the Europeans will press them to make concessions to the Palestinians. Earlier this week, community officials said they wanted to be "participants and not observers" in peace talks, but today they adopted the ambiguous position that they wanted to be "associated" with the conference. Mr Baker said he liked this formulation because "I like to have as many possibilities as I can" in seeking to persuade Israel and Arab countries to negotiate. Mr. Baker said he supported a community role at a peace conference. "We would like to see the approach to be one of inclusion rather than exclusion," he said.[38]

Israel is nervous about European participation in the "peace process," as well they might be. Israel is a key portion of Europe's Mediterranean ambitions. Following in the footsteps of Imperial Rome, the new Europe is expanding to the south, across the Mediterranean. First, the EC is being used as a model to create an African Common Market: "... the five countries of Africa's Maghreb region—Algeria, Libya, Mauritania, Morocco, and Tunisia—have set 1995 as the target date for the Union du Maghreb Arabe (UMA), the common market that they agreed to in principle last year."[39] Second, faced with the threat of unlimited immigration, the nations of southern Europe are attempting to clone the CSCE in North Africa and the Middle East to stabilize that region.

> Based on the so-called Helsinki process that helped ease East-West tensions over the last 15 years, Spain and Italy proposed today that a broad new organization be created to address security and development problems throughout the Mediterranean and the Middle East.... So far, preparations for a Conference on Security and Cooperation in the Mediterranean have involved Spain, Italy, Portugal and France in Europe, and Morocco, Tunisia, Algeria, Libya and Mauritania in North Africa. But the plan is that it eventually embrace other nations in Europe and the Middle East as well as the United States and the Soviet Union. Mr. De Michelis said that both Israel and the Palestine Liberation Organization would be invited to take part.... Spanish officials have said the purpose of the conference is not to resolve specific disputes in the region, but rather to establish a broad code of conduct covering a variety of problems, from the inviolability of

borders and democracy to immigrations and economic development.[40]

Perhaps the prophetic Middle East Peace Covenant addressed in Daniel 9:27 will come from just such a Conference organized by Europe and its evil prince. As we discussed earlier, the evil prince will observe the terms of the Covenant for only 3½ years, and then Israel will be oppressed. Given their recent heavy-handed dealings with Israel and their track record of questionable reliability, it is not hard to imagine a European betrayal of Israel in the middle of the Covenant's term. Even knowing this, given Israel's temporal dependence upon EC trade, Israel will see no other option than to dance to the devil's tune.

The similarities between the government of the new Europe and the prophetic kingdom of the evil prince are not accidental, and they will become increasingly similar as time passes. European integration is going to proceed according to God's timetable, and that timetable indicates increased rather than reduced speed.

We are living in momentous days. We are witnessing God's intervention in world events. He is personally executing His plans and bringing about the reign of His Messiah. As the world around us seems to be headed down the slippery slope of lawlessness, war, privation, and even global dictatorship that will attend man's final attempt at global management, it is good to know that the God of Israel, the Lord of Hosts, reigns.

Religion and the New Europe

Religion, during this reunification phase of European development, will be characterized by:

+ The initial predominance of the Roman Church.

* The eventual persecution of God's people.
* The destruction of the Roman Church by the evil prince's cabinet.
* The deification of the evil prince.

The role of the Roman Church in the development of European culture is influencing the early stages of European reunification. Those nations with the strongest affinity to the Roman Church more readily view themselves as European.

> History, geography, even religion condition the differing attitudes of the Twelve to the evolution of the EC. Catholic christendom imbued Europe, including part of what is now called Eastern Europe, with a feeling of unity until the end of the Middle Ages.... The fact that all members of the EC have Christian values in common, coupled with presumptions that democracy and free markets are the least bad ways of organizing society, are basic to their willingness to accept subservience to some common European law. But despite the instincts that Christians have in common, religion is also divisive within the EC. Largely-Protestant Danes, for instance, tend to think of the Community as "those Catholics down there," while the British Tories find it impossible to link up with the Christian Democratic group in the European Parliament partly because of the latter's Catholic overtones. Broadly speaking, Catholicism seems to have bred an acceptance of dirigisme. Protestantism tends toward self-reliance.... The Community inevitably draws some of its character from its core—six adjacent countries, largely sharing Catholicism and law based upon the Napoleonic code. Commission polls consistently show that the Britons,

Danes, Irish, Portuguese and the Dutch are less prone to think of themselves as "Europeans" than the seven other Community nations.[41]

Perhaps the supranational role that the Roman Church has played since the Middle Ages has primed these nations for the rebirth of European central government. The Church's influence on Europe is certainly not limited to the EC. With his persistent call for human rights and freedom, the Pope has been credited with the liberation of Eastern Europe.

As the new Europe takes shape, the Pope has been seeking to play a guiding role. He has been exhorting Europeans to forsake materialism and return to their spiritual roots—the Roman Church. However, his involvement in European affairs has not been universally accepted. When the Pope addressed the European Parliament, one of the Irish ministers shouted "Antichrist!" before being escorted out.

The Vatican Connection

Vatican City is a member of the CSCE and is using that organization to help mold the new Europe. Here are excerpts from Cardinal Agostino Casaroli's address to the 1990 Paris CSCE Summit:

Because the fate of Europe and her partners on the other side of the Atlantic affects the whole world, the participation of the Holy See ... in the proceedings of the CSCE becomes all the more understandable. Indeed, the Holy See is a power ... which is not only European, even though it does dispose of a very modest territory there—the Vatican City State—which allows it to exercise freely its universal mission. It is also a "power" actively involved throughout the world, in the fields of its proper competence, that is, in spiritual and moral matters, and consequently, too, in questions related to peace, the development of peoples and human rights.... The Holy See is all the more pleased to show its endorsement of the principles and commitments of the Helsinki Final Act and the Charter [of Paris for a New Europe] which we are going to sign, because it recognizes in them an echo of the Gospel message, with its moral values and its high spirituality which have shaped the soul of Europe and the regions to which she has handed down her ancient culture. These values also have much to say to other cultures.[42]

If the Roman Church truly is the mystery Babylon in Revelation 17, animosity between the forming European government and the Church will grow. We can initially expect that the Church will continue to enjoy an officially prominent position that will continue until the evil prince receives his full power. But even today, hatred for the Roman Church is growing at a grass-roots level:

New York's Cardinal John O'Connor singled out the press for deriding Catholics, like himself, "who dare to publicly uphold their faith." His contentions are supported by a major new study, "Media Coverage of the Catholic Church," to be released this week by The Center for Media and Public Affairs in Washington, D.C. Based on an analysis of the *New York Times*, the *Washington Post*, CBS Evening News and *Time* magazine over the last 30 years, the study finds that the church has been portrayed as "oppressive and anachronistic" and that media coverage has favored church critics over defenders.[43]

Even more virulent is the hatred being expressed by the radical gay community:

In the past 18 months or so, many churches across the country (six in Los Angeles alone) have been vandalized and broken into, with gay activists claiming responsibility. Masses and other religious ceremonies have been repeatedly disrupted, parishioners harassed and showered with condoms, and venomously anti-Catholic demonstrations conducted regularly outside churches.... I am talking about a straight-out hate campaign.... Savage mockery of Christianity is now a conventional part of the public gay culture. A ridiculous-looking Jesus figure carrying a cross is always featured in the gay Halloween parade in New York, along with the usual throng of hairy guys dressed as nuns. Some gay clubs and at least one gay movie feature a tableau of Jesus being sodomized.... Somehow the press has not gotten around to telling this story straight. For instance, an attempt by ACT UP to drown out an ordination ceremony in Boston was described rather carefully in the *Boston Globe* as "colorful, loud and peaceful." Readers were not told of the parody of the Communion rite that featured condoms as hosts, the mocking of Jesus's Sermon on the Mount as an endorsement of sodomy, the simulated anal and oral sex and the level of harassment outside the church.... The media are having unusual trouble describing gay attacks on Catholics.... Famous newspapers and commentators who scour language for the faintest hint of insensitivity to gays, blacks and women show little interest in this foot-stomping bigotry toward Catholics.[44]

As the Roman Church continues to confront the popular culture in the contentious areas of homosexuality, the role of women in the Church, abortion, etc., official support for the Church will wane. If the Roman Church tries to exert its preeminence over European Christendom, that will be its death knell. For it will be then that the evil prince and his cabinet of ten begin to rule Europe. They will not countenance any interference from an "archaic" religious organization, and will destroy her.

> ...these will hate the harlot and will make her desolate and naked, and will eat her flesh and will burn her up with fire (Revelation 17:16).

Revelation 18:9 tells us that those kings of the "old guard"—those hereditary kings and national leaders who have shared power with the Roman Church since the Middle Ages—will weep at her destruction. These kings and leaders will have lost their power to the prince's cabinet ministers, who will administer the planet.

Only then will the Pope's call be heeded; Europe will return to its spiritual roots. But those roots are not the Roman Church; instead, Europe will return to the Imperial Cult. They will abandon all pretense of Judeo-Christian tradition and will return to paganism and emperor worship.

> Then the king will do as he pleases, and he will exalt and magnify himself above every god, and will speak monstrous things against the God of gods (Daniel 11:36).

> Let no one in any way deceive you, for it will not come unless the apostasy comes first, and the man of lawlessness [the evil prince] is

revealed, the son of destruction, who opposes and exalts himself above every so-called god or object of worship, so that he takes his seat in the temple of God, displaying himself as being God (2 Thessalonians 2:3,4).

And there was given to him [the cabinet chief] to give breath to the image of the beast, that the image of the beast might even speak and cause as many as do not worship the image of the beast to be killed (Revelation 13:15).

During the reign of the evil prince, all who worship the one true God will be hunted down and murdered. In those days God's people will draw comfort from knowing that He is their salvation and their avenger, and that the days of the evil prince are numbered.

Back to a "Roman" Future

The pathway of Europe began in the days of Imperial Rome. Since the Germanic tribes precipitated the fall of Rome, there has been a near-continuous effort to reinstate central European government.

Today reunification efforts are being redoubled. In 1990 alone the three major European organizations—NATO, the CSCE, and the EC—initiated efforts to redesign themselves. These reconstruction efforts are not based upon past failure, like Soviet perestroika. Instead, these efforts are based upon an abundance of success. Europe is rebuilding its governmental organizations to expand the scope of its powers and to accommodate vastly increased membership.

The new Europe is conquering the world through economic seduction. No nation can resist her charms. Her flexible participation policies allow even the most skittish of nations to comfortably approach her. Once Europe's core organizations are restructured, it will not be long before she becomes a global government. After all, the world recognizes the need for global management, and Europe will be the only experienced, supranational organization which could easily step into that role.

In the not-too-distant future a charismatic young man will step up to lead Europe into its bright and glorious future. He will even be able to pave the uphill pathway to the milestone of the Middle East Peace Covenant. That man will be the evil prince. He and his management team will install global systems that will have this planet humming like a fine Swiss watch. Unfortunately, the world's undying gratitude will not be enough for this man; he will have himself deified. Anyone who does not participate in his worship and global management systems will be subject to his wrath. Just as in Imperial Rome, Judeo-Christians will be the only group who have problems with emperor worship and will face persecution and death. He will move European headquarters from Brussels to the "internationalized" city of Jerusalem, befitting his new global role. Instead of arriving at the milestone of the messianic kingdom, as they had anticipated, the world will find itself at the milestone of the kingdom of the evil prince.

From there the pathway of Europe will lead on, 3½ years later to the milestone of Armageddon. Here the usurper prince will do battle with the true King of Jerusalem—Messiah Jesus. It is in this final battle for world dominion that the evil prince will fall, and the pathway of Europe will abruptly end. All travelers who meet the Messiah's "visa requirements" will then proceed on the pathway of Israel...into the messianic kingdom.

We will all soon be traveling, either in the rapture to meet our Lord or into the realm of the evil prince. Both roads converge at the messianic kingdom, but they are far from equivalent. The rapture leads us immediately into our Lord's presence in the New Jerusalem. The pathway of Europe will lead through great trials, peril, and death.

Beloved in Jesus, remember that you are in the priesthood of the Most High God, the God of Israel. Use your office wisely and efficiently! Your "transfer" is being processed and time is short!

- Pray that the Holy Spirit will purify and prepare your heart for these final days before the Lord takes us home.

- Pray that the Holy Spirit will prepare the hearts of your loved ones to hear the message that God seeks to make peace with them, and has provided a Messiah for them.

- Pray that the words you share may take root that very day. If they do not, pray that the Lord would give your loved ones perfect recall, so they might remember your words when their hearts are ready.

- Pray that they might be protected from the spiritual deception that will come upon the world.

I believe, along with many others, that the rapture will occur before the Middle East Peace Covenant is signed. We know that the evil prince will be empowered after the first 3¹/₂ years of that Covenant have expired. Therefore, if the kingdom of the evil prince is as well-developed as we have seen, then is not our Lord almost at the door? Beloved, your Bridegroom comes!

5

THE
RUSSIAN
PATHWAY

|||||||||||||||||||||||||||| ✦ ||||||||||||||||||||||||||||

The Russian pathway is leading to a precipice. At the edge of that precipice is the milestone of the Russo-Israeli War. The footsteps on the ominous pathway ahead include hunger, privation, bankruptcy, civil unrest, dictatorship, oppression, and finally war. Tocqueville once said, "The most dangerous time for a bad government is when it starts to reform itself." This axiom is currently being proven in the former Soviet republics. As that massive nation breaks up and its population becomes increasingly paranoid and violent, the ability of its leaders to implement reform and exhibit rational behavior deteriorates.

The Russian pathway has been characterized by dictatorship and expansionism. These have been the twin goals of every ruler of Russia from the earliest czars to the current tenants in the Kremlin. These two goals are antithetical; that is, they ultimately collide. We have seen the result of this collision in our newspapers. Dictatorship robs a culture of its creativity and productivity. Successful expansionism requires a strong economic "bank" back home to draw upon. There is the conflict; the USSR was economically stagnating but continuing to finance the expansion of its territorial influence. Their financial bubble has finally burst!

After decades of financially propping up the regimes that they have sponsored throughout the world, as well as their own economy, foreclosure day finally approached. Like many bankrupt corporations, just before their demise the Soviets attempted a corporate restructuring which they called "perestroika." But this was too little too late. As their economy imploded, they were unable or unwilling to restructure the nation quickly enough to stay ahead of the blast. And as all desperate people facing mass annihilation, they now proceed not judiciously but instinctively. The former Soviet peoples will ultimately return to their unsuccessful but familiar method of governance: dictatorship and expansionism.

Accompanying this nostalgic return to the past will be an attempt to recapture some of the losses. That may be the inspiration for the biblical Russo-Israeli War described in Ezekiel 38 and 39. Such a war could please what remains of the Soviet military, appease its neglected Arab clients, and be launched under the pretext of reclaiming Soviet Jewry and the mythical goods they may be accused of taking with them. As soon as the Russians hatch and begin to execute this scheme, the Russian pathway will come to an abrupt end at the hands of God Himself.

The Early Russian Pathway

In the ninth century the geographical area recently governed by the USSR was invaded by Germanic tribes from the north, known to the Byzantines as the "Rus" or "Rhos." They sold the original Slavic inhabitants into slavery. They used trade, piracy, colonization, and their skillful military use of longships on key European rivers to expand their borders and influence.[1] Thus began a long tradition of brutal oppression and expansionism.

In 1462 the Slavic Grand Duke of Moscow, Ivan the Great, ascended to the Russian throne. The czars (caesars) ruled Russia until 1917, and continued the tradition of the "Rus": oppression and expansion. The expansion of Russia's borders almost beyond the point of defensibility brought increased paranoia. Supporting a military force large enough to patrol so vast a perimeter and engage in active warfare strained Russian resources.

Near the end of the World War I, in a cycle of events not unlike today, the czarist government could not adequately supply its troops and keep its factories and railways running, nor could it feed its people and control prices. Amid riots, strikes, desertions, and calls for reform, the Czar abdicated. A provisional government of liberal democrats and socialists was formed in March 1917. This government sought to form a permanent democratic government, created local workers' councils ("soviets"), immediately freed political prisoners, and guaranteed civil liberties. Unfortunately, it did not concentrate on feeding the population and reforming land ownership. Rather, the new government concentrated its resources on continuing the war.

The Bolsheviks, led by Lenin and Trotsky, tugged at the heartstrings of the hungry Soviet masses with the promise of "peace, bread, and land." They quickly gained influence over the local "soviets," and in November 1917 Red troops wrested control from the provisional government. The Bolsheviks accepted German terms and forfeited Finland, the Baltic states, Poland, and the Ukraine. They immediately turned to domestic affairs and nationalized industry and land ownership. All opposition was brutally crushed.

The Russian economy was in a shambles. The war had destroyed many farms and factories. Management and workers alike lacked skill and motivation. In 1921 Lenin introduced the "New Economic Policy"—the forerunner of perestroika. This scheme relaxed Communist principles and allowed for store managers to own their stores, for farmers to own and sell their surplus crops, and for foreigners to invest and gain technical employment in Russia. This policy was successful in putting Russia back on its feet.

Lenin's death in 1924 was followed by a succession of Communist dictators: Stalin, Khrushchev, Brezhnev, Chernenko, and Andropov. During much of that time, goals for the Russian economy were set by multi-year plans. These plans established Russian heavy industry and state control of agriculture at the cost of several million lives. They also institutionalized waste and bureaucracy. Russia became a world supplier of heavy industrial products, such as military equipment, but could not supply itself with enough food or consumer goods.

Perestroika and Glasnost

Little has changed. The republics of the former Soviet Union still cannot supply themselves with food and consumer goods, and their economies are in a death spiral. In 1985 Mikhail Gorbachev came to power. It has been said that the KGB had studied the Soviet economy and recognized that it was fast reaching the point of no return. The theory goes that perestroika ("restructuring") and glasnost ("openness") were conjured up by party loyalists, like Mr. Gorbachev, to pull the USSR back from the fast approaching brink. This scheme was very similar to Lenin's "New Economic Policy": They both relaxed ideological control of production and management.

One of the first things CEO Gorbachev did for his ailing corporation was to divest its unprofitable subsidiaries: He released Soviet control over Eastern Europe and took Communist regimes worldwide off the dole. That cut off a major outflow of capital.

The next thing he undertook was to woo the West. His economy could no longer afford the arms race, so his gambit was to convince the West that the Soviet Union was a good neighbor, and that they should lay down their weapons. So the leader of the Communist world appeared on the Western doorstep, flushed from a recent transformation akin to a religious conversion. His smiles and populist style won Western hearts. This well-studied man said everything they wanted to hear with apparent deep conviction. He was quite different from the cold, imposing lookalikes who had recently held the Russian "throne."

Mr. Gorbachev frequently spoke of his vision for a "common European house." He was not happy about the continued existence of NATO. In that the Warsaw Pact died with his divestiture of Eastern Europe, he very much wanted to see NATO immediately supplanted by the CSCE or some other pan-European security organization. Among the outcast cynics there were suspicions that underlying his thinking was the dream that a *European* security organization would *include* the USSR, which partially lies on the European continent, and *exclude* the Americas. This would allow the ever-hopeful Soviets to regain their position of power in Europe as soon as they dealt with their economic cataclysm.

Vendula Kubalkova, professor of international studies at the University of Miami, has said, "When Gorbachev allowed the Eastern European countries to have their revolutions, at the back of his mind I think he knew he could use their integration with the rest of Europe as an entry to a more convenient arrangement: this all-European Security system he talks about, modeled... on the CSCE.... Gorbachev's repeated references to a common European home reflect a Soviet desire to capitalize on pro-integration sentiment that is running high.... The Soviets will play up the emotional pull of a post-Cold War, reunited European continent not only to maximize Soviet fortunes, but to minimize the role of the West.... The new Pan-European security structure Gorbachev mentions evolving out of CSCE will eventually exclude the United States and Canada."[2]

Yet Western leaders were unsuspecting. Presidents Gorbachev and Bush as well as their foreign ministers Shevardnadze and Baker became fast friends. Together in friendship, they would forge a new world. The original Bush vision for a New World Order was one of a post-Cold War superpower alliance operating through the rejuvenated U.N. leading the world into an age of peace. This vision had one overwhelming flaw: It assumed that the Soviet Union would continue to be a superpower.

After much success on the foreign affairs circuit, which even included winning a Nobel Peace Prize, Gorbachev first became a prisoner of his nation's domestic plagues. Later he would become a literal prisoner of his own cabinet. Recent events in the former Soviet republics are increasingly grim. They characterize a people on the verge of complete governmental, economic, and societal collapse.

Plagues of Dissent

The USSR was a union of 15 republics. "The 15 republics are not the only divisions within the Soviet Union. There are also 20 'autonomous republics,' eight 'autonomous regions' and ten 'autonomous areas.' These are inhabited by smaller ethnic minorities, such as the Tartars in Russia, the Abkhazians in Georgia and, most explosively, the Armenians in the Nagorno-Kakabakh autonomous region of Azerbaijan. Autonomous republics have their own parliaments and laws."[3]

When the USSR was ruled by a central iron fist, dissent was beyond thought. However, with the introduction of glasnost, the republics and other nationalist movements were emboldened. They watched and noted as Eastern Europe was released by the Soviet central government. Although those nations were fumbling, they were making serious efforts to restructure their economies, societies, and governments. If they failed, it was because they had been given the freedom to do so. In 1989 the Soviet republics began actively seeking autonomy from the central government. The failed coup of August 1991 hastened their independence.

Tensions between these republics and their indigenous tribal groups have frequently erupted into violence. The unpredictability and violence of these nationalists was a source of great consternation for their former Soviet masters. *Newsweek* reported on April 9, 1990, that "Moscow was worried enough during the recent turmoil in Azerbaijan to send regular army units to reinforce KGB guards at nuclear sites there." Subsequent reports indicated that the central government moved much of its nuclear arsenal into the Russian Republic for fear that these arms could fall into militant nationalist hands.

To stem the tide of governmental disintegration, President Gorbachev had called for "a new union treaty." This new treaty was intended to redefine the powers of the Kremlin and the republics. "The republics could be something more like sovereign states, while remaining in the Soviet Union. The grip of the central planners in Moscow would be broken, and the Kremlin left with power only over such things as defense and monetary policy. And, because the republics would choose whether or not to sign the treaty, Mr. Gorbachev hopes that the country, held together by choice rather than coercion, would not merely survive, but emerge the stronger."[4] Having had a taste of freedom from an oppressive central government, agreement on a new union treaty was elusive. Initial drafts of this treaty, prepared by the

Kremlin, gave all significant power to the central government, and what was left to the republics—an offer that was easily refused.

It is interesting to note that in 1991 the USSR and the European Community were concurrently rewriting their constitutions. Both unions were facing membership problems, but the problems were inverted! On the one hand the Soviet republics were trapped inside "Fortress Russia" and clamoring to get out. On the other hand, many nations feared being trapped outside of "Fortress Europe" and were clamoring to get in!

Eventually the central government redrafted its union treaty, in which critical powers were ceded to the republics. The signing of this treaty was intentionally preempted by the August 1991 coup. Had the coup succeeded, the republics would have lost the modest gains that they had made.

As the coup failed, the republics seized the opportunity to declare their independence. They were then left with the impossible task of administering a bankrupt economy and attempting to implement painful market reforms. The resulting privation will eventually erupt in civil unrest. If the Communist hard-liners turn this disorder to their advantage and stage another coup, as the prophet Ezekiel appears to indicate that they will, Russia will have a cold-blooded, genocidal dictator once again at its helm.

Economic Plagues

The economic distress in the former Soviet republics is almost unimaginable. The people are faced with severe shortages of food, fuel, consumer goods, and housing.

Despite a bumper crop in the fields, farmers lack the fuel, machinery, parts, and labor to harvest their own grain. The farmers have threatened that "unless the city people help in the vegetable fields, they will not get a single gram of food."[5] The situation is increasingly desperate. "Over the past few months food supplies have dwindled steadily throughout the country, leaving many store shelves bare and increasing popular dissatisfaction.... The main agricultural daily *Selskaya Zhizn* said that the state was not buying enough grain to ensure steady bread supplies to the population. The newspaper said that the state had to acquire 85.3 million tons of grain, but that only 76 million had been contracted."[6]

With farm production down, the Soviets have historically looked abroad to supplement their own harvest. However, in 1990 a severe shortage of hard currency hampered foreign grain and agricultural equipment purchases. In addition, they fell behind in their bill payments, thus ruining their credit with Western banks. In a move of desperation, the government began selling off "the family jewels" just to make it through another day. There were reports that the Soviet government had sold a billion dollars' worth of gold, platinum, palladium, diamonds, and other metals. On July 26, 1990, it was reported that the government had made a deal with one of the world's leading diamond traders, DeBeers of South Africa. In this five-year agreement, the Soviets were to sell off 5 billion dollars' worth of uncut diamonds, and DeBeers immediately advanced the Soviets a billion dollars in cash.

In mid-1991 the American intelligence community submitted a dismal annual report on the state of the Soviet economy:

> The economy of the Soviet Union faces a decline in output of 10 percent, an inflation rate exceeding 100 percent, and the likelihood of a "radically worse" year.... The intelligence agencies

envisioned various scenarios in which the government of President Mikhail S. Gorbachev either succeeded in mediating the worst differences between the central government and restive Soviet republics or failed and turned to more repressive measures. Even in the best case—with improvement in relations between the central government and the republics and a renewal of reform efforts—the study says Soviet output would "probably still fall some 10 percent." In the worst case, repressive steps "to control the republics, to enforce state orders and to stabilize the economy" would speed "the downward spiral," it says. In that case, the study says, "the decline would eventually equal or exceed the 30 percent drop in GNP and the 25 percent unemployment rate experienced in the United States during the Great Depression of 1930-1933.[7]

The abject poverty and state of frustration currently being experienced by the former Soviet peoples will have three direct effects:

- It will soften their resolve, and make them willing to accept a dictator offering messianic promises and hopes for returning to "the good old days."

- It will set them off on a witch-hunt to find the culprits responsible for their suffering.

- It will prepare them for war. Their new leadership will be more than happy to provide the angry and vengeful population with an external outlet for their hostility—Israel.

Societal Plagues

As the food grows scarce, anti-Semitism becomes more virulent:

> Food shortages, unemployment, economic crisis—all of these in any country exacerbate racism. That the Jews are blamed in the Soviet Union for the fact that the shelves are empty does not surprise them. One young Jewish woman said: "We're supposed to have eaten all the food, all their food. No food, blame the Jews; no cigarettes, blame the Jews; no anything, blame the Jews."... In an interview in the *New York Times* magazine last January, Valentine Rasputin, a member of Gorbachev's Presidential Council, said: "I think today the Jews here should feel responsible for the sin of having carried out the [Bolshevik] revolution and for the shape it took. They should feel responsible for the terror that existed during the revolution. They played a large role and their guilt is great." Mr. Rasputin, it should be recalled, was appointed by Mr. Gorbachev. Jews and human rights activists are troubled by this and by the fact that at no time has President Gorbachev publicly denounced anti-Semitism.[8]

So far the Soviet Union has issued visas to approximately one million Jews who are voluntarily seeking to emigrate. Of those, Israel is expected to have received 500,000 by the end of 1991. Israel is having great difficulty housing the flood of Soviet Jews that arrive each month in what they term "Operation Exodus." As a result of this great influx of people, many Israelis are now living in tents. *Jewish Press* reports indicate that the current voluntary emigration may soon become a forced expulsion. This would somewhat relieve Soviet shortages and put additional pressure on Israel.

Soviet Gentiles were interested in getting in on this Exodus as well, but they're not necessarily interested in wandering to the literal Promised Land. It is ironic to note that the anti-Semitic Ukrainians have been forging Jewish birth certificates.

> For centuries, the people of the Ukraine were renowned for the virulence of their anti-Semitism. Now their descendants are queuing up to buy what, in an earlier age, would have amounted to a death warrant—a Jewish birth certificate. Evidence of Jewish birth is now a passport to the West. In the Ukraine, where some of the worst massacres of Jews under the Nazi occupation took place—especially at Babi Yar near the capital, Kiev—people are paying huge sums for forged documents showing that they have Jewish origins. The last thing these newly-converted "Jews" want is to emigrate to Israel. They long to go to Germany, which has stated that it has a moral duty to allow Jews to settle there once more.[9]

This mass emigration made the Soviet establishment uncomfortable. They realized that people are valuable resources. Their two-legged diamonds in the rough are hopping onto anything with wings or wheels that will carry them away from the former Soviet republics.

> Just when the country needs them most, tens of thousands of the Soviet Union's best minds are streaming to the West in what the officials describe as a brain drain so massive that it could jeopardize the Kremlin's reforms. The

current tidal wave of emigration, expected to total more than half a million this year, is carrying off the very people needed to rebuild the nation, according to Soviet authorities, who say that the exodus could also set back their country's scientific research for decades. ... The outflow of Soviet talent—an estimated 20 percent of emigrants hold advanced or professional degrees—has become so noticeable that President Mikhail S. Gorbachev himself has complained about it.[10]

This does not bode well for Soviet Jews who are building their dreams in the land of milk and honey. If the Jews continue to be cast as the source of Soviet ills, and are thought to have escaped those ills, one can easily see how the Russian people would be willing to initiate the Russo-Israeli War.

With no hope and no vision for the future, and with spirits seething with jealousy, envy, hatred, and violence, the hearts of the Soviet people are being hardened for judgment on the hills of Judea.

The Coup of 1991

As the day dawned in Moscow on August 19, 1991, Soviet citizens awoke to find that President Gorbachev had been "taken ill." Suspicions were aroused immediately. As the old Russian joke goes: "Ill? I hadn't even heard that he had been arrested!"

In fact, Gorbachev *had* been arrested and the central government had fallen to a hard-line putsch. The rebellion was led by an "emergency committee" comprised of eight members of Gorbachev's own government. This rogues' gallery of Communist xenophobes included:

V.S. Pavlov:	Prime Minister of the USSR, leader of the "legislative coup," an unsuccessful hard-liner attempt to wrest power from Gorbachev through the Soviet Parliament.
G.I. Yanayev:	Acting President of the USSR, ex-Vice President under the Gorbachev administration, the "stand-up guy" who saw no problems with Pavlov's legislative coup.
V.A. Kryuchkov:	Chairman of the KGB.
B.K. Pugo:	Interior Minister of the USSR.
D.T. Yazov:	Defense Minister of the USSR.
O.D. Baklanov:	First Deputy Chairman of the USSR Defense Council.
V.A. Starodubtsev:	Chairman of the Farmers' Union of the USSR.
A.I. Tizyakov:	President of the Association of State Enterprises and Industrial, Construction, Transport, and Communications Facilities of the USSR.

These men sought a pretense of legality for their acts of treason and treachery. They "constitutionally" elevated their front man and Gorbachev's hand-picked Vice President, Gennadi Yanayev, to the position of Acting President upon concocting Gorbachev's alleged illness.

These men—epitomes of the Old Communist Order—and men of their ilk have ruled the Soviet Union with an iron fist since the Bolshevik Revolution in 1917. They felt very threatened as Gorbachev prepared to return to Moscow on Tuesday to sign a new Union Treaty with the Soviet republics. This Treaty would have devolved much of the power of the central government, *their* power, to the republics:

- The President of the new "Union of Soviet Sovereign Republics" would have been directly elected to a limited term by popular vote.

- The republics would have gained political power, including the appointment of one house of the federal legislature which would have been able to veto federal laws and the creation of a constitutional court which would have allowed republics to suspend and dispute federal law, and even secede.

- International relations would have been shared, with the central government providing a coordinated foreign policy and the republics freely conducting their own diplomatic and commercial relations.

- Although control of the military and the republics' security forces would have remained under the control of the central government, their use would be restricted inside the country.

- Economic power would have been divided between the central government and the republics, including the control of natural resources, taxation, energy, key industries, and transportation.

Fatal Miscalculations

For these men who have ruled with an iron fist, the disorder which glasnost introduced was ruinous and anathema, and this Treaty was viewed as a death sentence to their way of life. So, principally to preempt the signing of this Treaty and restore the old order, the military coup of 1991 was launched.

From the very beginning, it began to unravel. The coconspirators made several fatal mistakes.

In the early hours of the coup Gorbachev was arrested, but the popular and popularly elected Yeltsin was not. Belatedly, the conspirators sent tanks to encircle the Russian Parliament Building. Few Russians have given a rat's eyelash for Gorbachev, but they were willing to lay their bodies in front of tanks to defend Yeltsin. In fact, Yeltsin even found support in the military. Many of the tanks and armored personnel carriers which initially surrounded the Parliament Building switched sides and ended up defending him. By not seizing Yeltsin in the first moments of the coup, thus allowing him to rally the Russian people and the international community, a fatal mistake was made.

Usually when a coup is launched, the military is moving into key positions concurrently with the announcement of the "change in leadership." Troops did not move into Moscow until four hours after Gorbachev's arrest—a second fatal mistake.

Another blunder involved the makeup of the troops sent to Moscow. Instead of using loyal troops from the Asian republics, the conspirators used conscripted Russian troops, many of whom voted for Yeltsin and who had family in the Moscow crowds. This division of loyalty resulted in a split in the military—another fatal mistake.

If these coup leaders truly represent the finely tuned apparatus of oppression in the Soviet Union, why weren't they more organized? These men looked like "The gang who couldn't shoot straight"!

There is speculation that these men *had* developed a carefully laid plan. This theory continues that Gorbachev was tipped off and tried to return to Moscow on Monday rather than Tuesday, and therefore the trap was sprung prematurely. This theory explains away the fatal mistakes made by the conspirators: Their timetable was blown and key players were not in place.

It is said that Machiavelli once advised, "If you are going to strike at a king, you must be sure to kill him." Well, the "emergency committee" members were never serious students of Western culture. They shrank from killing Gorbachev and Yeltsin. As the coup collapsed, Gorbachev and Yeltsin were back—and angry.

In the wake of the coup there was a countercoup. Although Gorbachev was "back in power" he operated almost as a Yeltsin puppet. Yeltsin and the radical reformers began conducting a typical Soviet purge of their own. The conspirators were arrested and charged with treason. The Communist Party was dissolved. Party newspapers, including *Pravda*, were shut and subsequently "reorganized." Central government officials were purged and replaced with radical reformers.

Under the guise of "democracy and reform," the Soviet Union experienced a second putsch, this time not from the right but from the left. The elimination of opposing parties, the limitation of communication, and the arrest and replacement of government officials were all objectives of both putsches. The left wing radical reformers had come out on top, but the power structure in the Soviet Union remained in a state of extreme flux. In late 1991 the central government was officially dissolved and replaced by the new Commonwealth of Independent States.

The More Things Change...

Before the coup Gorbachev was locally unpopular because he had shown bad judgment when selecting government officials, the government was bankrupt, the international community was afraid to invest in an unstable nation, there were no food or consumer goods on the shelves, there was a housing crisis, the cities were leftist while the countryside was rightist, ethnic hatred frequently erupted into local warfare, crime was rampant, the government was bureaucratically paralyzed, fuel supplies were low, and winter was coming.

It was due to these desperate conditions that the coup leaders believed that the people would be willing to return to the "good old days"—no freedom, but fixed prices and government provision. They were wrong, because the people were not desperate enough...yet. As every comedian knows, the two secrets of success are *timing* and *timing*. This was the key element that the coup lacked.

Although the Soviet central government has been replaced by a Commonwealth, a truly stable government has not emerged. The seeds of revolution still grow in the Soviet republics. The elation that the Soviet people experienced in their "victory over Communism" will only deepen their despair and disappointment as their privation worsens. There may yet be revolution; it is not over!

The Soviets and the Middle East

In 1948, when Israel declared its statehood, the Soviet Union was one of the first nations to recognize it. Apart from the fact that the Soviets expected Israel to have a sympathetic socialist government in the Middle East, they also enjoyed tormenting the British, who had had no end of problems administering the area. Just as the thrill was beginning to fade, they discovered that the U.S., with its large Jewish population, would always be locked into supporting Israel. This left the lucrative Arab playing field wide open for the Soviets. Yes, life was worth living once again. For additional jollies and points with their Arab friends they would harass their own Jewish communities.

Syria

With the Soviet economy geared almost exclusively for the production of heavy military equipment, the Soviet Union looked to the Middle East for clientele and found a rich and fertile market. In the 1960's the Soviets helped install a radical Syrian government. From the 60's through the 80's Syria was a major base of Soviet troublemaking in the Middle East.

> 1970—Syrian-backed Palestinians attempted to overthrow the Jordanian government.

> 1976—Syrian-backed factions began dismembering Lebanon, and finally succeeded in installing a Syrian regime in 1990.

> 1978—Syria condemned Egypt for signing the Camp David Accords with Israel.

> 1980—Syria backed Iran in the eight-year Iran-Iraq war.

Syria had dreams of creating "Greater Syria," and the Soviets would have loved to help make their dreams come true. But then perestroika arrived and Syria was one of the unprofitable subsidiaries that the Soviets divested. Since that time Syria has been moving into the Western camp, as evidenced by its participation in the coalition against Iraq. Her terrorist activities, if not stopped, are at least less overt.

Egypt

Egypt had also been a Soviet client. The Soviets financed Nasser's new war machine which he used against

Israel in the 1967 War. Soviet advisers remained in
Egypt until Egyptian President Sadat threw them out
after the disastrous Yom Kippur War in 1973.

Iraq

Iraq was also a Soviet client. Iraq was armed with
Soviet equipment and assisted by Soviet advisers throughout the Gulf War. So closely were the two nations militarily allied that Iraq's defeat was considered a humiliation for the Soviet Army.

Iran

Under the Shah, Iran was allied with the West. When
the Ayatollahs took over, both the U.S. and the USSR
were viewed as imperialist "satanic" enemies. But in the
post-Gulf era, things have changed.

> *Newsweek* has learned that Iran and the Sov-
> iet Union have begun to forge a closer military
> partnership.... But sources say that on Janu-
> ary 3, at least 50 Iranian military officers
> began training at a naval base in the Baltic
> coast city of Riga, Latvia, site of recent unrest
> between independence-minded Latvians and
> Soviet troops.... The likeliest reason for this
> sudden cooperation between the two countries
> is that both are hedging bets on alignments
> once the Persian Gulf War is over.[11]

Radical Moslem Nations

Soviet Arabism went beyond the military cash regis-
ter. The former Soviet Union had a very large Moslem
population which stretched along its southern flank.

Since the fall of the central government, these republics have achieved nation status and are forming alliances with surrounding Arab nations.

The Gulf War split the Arab community in two: those who joined the coalition, and the anti-West, radical Arab nations. This latter group includes Libya, Sudan, Ethiopia, and Iran. Not only would they gladly join in a war against Israel, but they are the very Arab nations whom Ezekiel has prophesied would do just that! Throughout the Gulf War the Soviet Union cast its obligatory votes at the U.N. to pacify the West, but it also held fast to its Arab alliances and did nothing that would damage them in the postwar world. Russia will call in those markers when they issue their call to war against their common enemy, Israel.

Russia: New Age Egypt

For the past 70 years the Soviets have been a godless nation, spreading terror throughout the nations of the world. For the past 70 years the American Christian right seems to have demonstrated a greater fear of the Soviet Union than faith that her godlessness would bring her to judgment. The fall of the Soviet Union should come as no surprise to Bible students.

Just as the ancient Egyptians were afflicted by plagues so that their hearts might be hardened, so Russia appears to have been afflicted. Just as the ancient Egyptians devised an evil plan to expel the Jews and then follow after them to destroy them, so Russia appears to be following in the same path. Just as God brought about the destruction of Pharaoh's army so that the Egyptians would "know that I am the Lord," so we are told in Ezekiel 38 that the armies of Russia and her allies will be destroyed by God to "make Myself known in the sight of many nations; and they will know that I am the Lord" (v. 23).

6

THE
ARAB/MOSLEM
PATHWAY

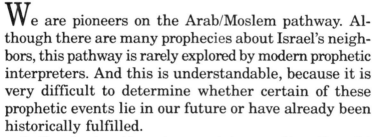

We are pioneers on the Arab/Moslem pathway. Although there are many prophecies about Israel's neighbors, this pathway is rarely explored by modern prophetic interpreters. And this is understandable, because it is very difficult to determine whether certain of these prophetic events lie in our future or have already been historically fulfilled.

In the nineteenth century certain expositors thought that many of the prophecies about Israel were fulfilled by the church. They could not envision that God would literally regather Israel after two millennia of exile. But when God began regathering Israel in 1948, these interpretive errors had to be corrected.

Today many biblical commentaries interpret the vast body of Moslem/Arab prophecies to have been historically fulfilled. But a close examination of these prophecies indicates that many of them may apply to current or future events.

The nation of Israel is surrounded by "relatives"—some close, some distant, most hostile. These tribal nations are predominantly Moslem. Although we tend to think of all Middle Eastern nations as being Arab, few if any of these nations are technically of "Arab" origin.

The Arab/Moslem pathway began with the migration and settlement of ancient family groups. In time this pathway was dominated by a long succession of empires—some local, some "foreign." As each new empire grew in size and military power, it would conquer and replace its predecessor. The Bible describes the birth and demise of many of these familial nations. Many of these nations face severe judgment in the near future because of their treatment of Israel.

The Arab/Moslem pathway has become a "divided highway"; the path has split into a "radical lane" and a "moderate lane." On the "radical lane" we find two groups: 1) Iran (Persia), Ethiopia/Sudan (Cush), Libya (Put); and 2) Iraq (Babylon), Jordan (Moab, Ammon, Edom), and Saudi Arabia (Arabia).

Earlier in this book we discussed the judgment of "Group 1" when they will cast their lots with Russia during the Russo-Israeli War. We will not address them again here. Those nations in "Group 2" are either being judged or will soon be judged.

On the "moderate lane" we find Egypt and more recently Assyria. The future of these nations is quite interesting and not what you might expect.

Empires in the Middle East

From her earliest days, Israel has had a tenuous relationship with her neighbors. God has more than once used these surrounding nations to conquer and punish Israel for her unfaithfulness. In fact, Israel was ruled and oppressed by these Gentile nations from the fall of Jerusalem to the Babylonians in 586 B.C. until it declared its independence in 1948 A.D. This domination has been in the form of a long succession of empires which have ruled not only Israel but the entire Middle East at one time or another.

Major Empires Dominating the Middle East		
Assyrian Empire	1100 B.C. –	625 B.C.
New Babylonian (Chaldean) Empire	625 B.C. –	539 B.C.
Persian Empire	550 B.C. –	331 B.C.
Alexander's (Greek) Empire	336 B.C. –	146 B.C.
Roman Empire	264 B.C. –	565 A.D.
Byzantine Empire	4th C A.D. –	1453 A.D.
Moslem Empire	622 A.D. –	10th C A.D.
Turkish (Ottoman) Empire	11th C A.D. –	1914 A.D.
British Empire & France	1914 A.D. –	1960's A.D.

Rather than attempt to review all of these empires, we will concentrate our attention on the last three—the Moslem, Turkish, and European empires. These empires have the greatest bearing on our world today.

The Moslem Empire

Islam was introduced to the nations of the Middle East by Mohammed at the beginning of the seventh century. The belief that dying while fighting for the faith would assure entrance into Paradise made the Moslems mighty warriors. It was this common faith which forged the Moslem Empire.

In the seventh and eighth centuries, the imperialist Moslem Empire vastly expanded. It annexed Israel and Syria in the north; Iran, Iraq and northwest India in the east; and North Africa, Spain, and parts of France in the west. The Moslem invasion of Europe was stopped by Charles Martel, King of the Franks, at the Battle of Tours in 732.

The Moslem Empire was the center of cultural advancement, standing in stark contrast with the European "Dark Ages." While the Roman Church was torturing and murdering European academicians for the sin of natural curiosity and free thought, the Moslems were—

- ◆ founding many great universities;
- ◆ preserving the achievements of classical culture;
- ◆ making advances in agriculture, architecture, mathematics, and medicine.

Whereas European "Christians" tortured and murdered "unbelievers," the early Moslems did not forcibly convert indigenous populations. However, the appeal of Paradise as a reward for righteous living, plus exemption from a tax levied only on unbelievers, was enough to convert many people to the Moslem faith.

Sequel to the Moslem Empire

By the tenth century the Moslem Empire began to disintegrate into independent Moslem kingdoms. In the eleventh century the Moslem Seljuk Turks seized Baghdad and dominated the Middle East. Two centuries later their leadership role shifted to the Ottoman Turks. This Turkish domination of "Arab" land for almost a millennium is the root cause of the diplomatic problems between Turkey and her Moslem neighbors today.

As the Turks continued to expand their influence, their neighbors became increasingly nervous. During the late eleventh century the Byzantine emperor appealed to the Roman Church for military assistance.

The Roman Church viewed this plea as an opportunity to liberate the Holyland from Moslem control. It was in response to this appeal that the Crusades were launched. The Crusades were a Christian "holy war," or, as the Moslems call it, a *jihad*. During the First Crusade the European army gained control of Jerusalem and parts of the Holyland. A hundred years later the Moslems, led by Saladin, retook the Holyland. Despite additional Crusades, Israel remained part of the Ottoman Empire until the end of World War I in 1918.

By the nineteenth century the Ottoman Empire became known as the "sick man of Europe." The Turkish government had become corrupt, inefficient, and religiously oppressive. Many of the nations which suffered under its domination began to press for independence. Competition for control of the Balkans brought Turkey and Russia into confrontation. In 1914 Turkey entered World War I on the side of the Central Powers (Germany and Austria-Hungary), primarily motivated by her hatred for Russia. With the defeat of the Central Powers at the end of World War I, the Treaty of Lausanne provided for Turkey to retain Asia Minor, Constantinople, and the Dardanelles, but to lose all non-Turkish territory.

In 1920 the Supreme War Council granted Britain and France mandates to administer lands in the Middle East. Britain was given control of areas which subsequently became known as Iraq, Jordan, and Israel. France was given control of territories which subsequently became Lebanon and Syria. The borders of these emerging nations were drawn rather arbitrarily and did not conform to any historical or ethnic boundaries. It was this questionable process of nation building which—

- encouraged Saddam Hussein to "question the sovereignty" of Kuwait;

- ◆ left the Kurds homeless and living as out-
  casts in Turkey, Syria, and Iraq;

- ◆ created a "Palestinian state"—the Hashem-
  ite Kingdom of Jordan—in the land originally promised to Israel.

People in general have long memories and families
have even longer ones. The Middle East's long history of
domination and oppression has spawned much of the
hostility and mistrust that we are witnessing today.

Today...

- ◆ the Arabs claim ownership of Israel based
  upon their conquest between the seventh
  and tenth centuries.

- ◆ the Arabs dislike the Turks because of Turkish domination during the Ottoman Empire.

- ◆ the Arabs distrust the Iranians, although
  they are fellow Moslems because they are
  Persian and not Arab.

- ◆ the Arabs and Israelis distrust the Europeans because of the Crusades and European colonialism after World War I.

Today the Middle East is like the world's most contentious "family gathering." It has brawling brothers,
knock-down-drag-out inheritance fights, thieving cousins, petty bickering, religious arguments, and grudge
matches that outlive their originators. The only thing
upon which they can agree is their hatred for the family
black sheep—Israel. And as with every family gathering that turns violent, soon the police will be called in.

While the "world's police" share this family's contempt for Israel, the world's Judge does not. As we have

discussed in previous chapters, we will soon be seeing the "world's police" negotiating and possibly imposing a Middle East Peace Treaty. This peace treaty will not secure Israel's future. However, Israel has a Judge looking out for her interests. That Judge has reviewed how each of these "family members" has treated Israel, and has already passed judgment on them. It is possible that those judgments have already begun to be meted out.

The Judgment of Babylon/Iraq

We know how the war began and how it will end. We are still fuzzy about the middle part.

—Israeli Deputy Foreign Minister
Benjamin Netanyahu[1]

Everyone watched the Gulf War and knows how it started. After a hundred hours of ground action, everyone believes they know how it ended. Oh, yes, there's some humanitarian work to be done with the Kurds, but nonetheless, the war is over and the world rejoices.

The Fall of Modern Babylon?

We who live in Western society live in a fast-forward reality. We want fast action and immediate closure. We have learned from our video screens that problems can develop and be solved in 120 minutes, given the casting of the appropriate cinematic hero, such as General Norman Schwartzkopf. While General Schwartzkopf is a hero of Cecil B. DeMille proportions, we would be very naive to believe that he has secured a lasting peace and that we have heard the last of Saddam Hussein.

One hint that the war is not truly over may be found in the prophetic Word. The prophet Jeremiah may have alluded to this break in the action when he wrote:

> Thus says the Lord of hosts, the God of Israel:
> "The daughter of Babylon is like a threshing
> floor at the time it is stamped firm; yet in a
> little while the time of harvest will come for
> her" (Jeremiah 51:33).

Another hint that the war may not be over appeared
in the April 28, 1991, *New York Times*:

> ...as long as President Saddam Hussein of
> Iraq remains in power, the war is not over in
> the eyes of the Arabs or Israelis, and both still
> have their eyes more on him than each other.

There is strong circumstantial and prophetic evidence that we are witnessing the fall of Babylon. The
period through which we are now living may just be a
seventh inning stretch before a cataclysmic judgment.
This is the "fuzzy middle part." It is too early to be
certain, but if the final judgment of Babylon is in progress, then this war will be a watershed event, for it will
set up the fulfillment of many other prophecies. Hussein
may be correct in labeling this war "the mother of all
battles," for it may be the forerunner of the Russo-
Israeli War and Armageddon itself.

Prophetic Conditions

The area occupied by the ancient Babylonians and
Chaldeans is now in modern Iraq. The primary prophetic texts dealing with the fall of Babylon are found in
Jeremiah 50 and 51, and Isaiah 13. Before looking at the
similarity between the morning news and these prophecies, it is important to first discuss events to which these
prophecies do *not* refer.

First, I do not believe that these passages in Jeremiah
and Isaiah are referring to the ancient fall of Babylon

because of the inconsistencies between the historical facts and the vision described by the prophets.

In its first fall, Babylon was conquered by a single empire—Medo-Persia. In the prophetic Word we are told that it will be encircled by many nations from "the farthest horizons." The prophets also describe Babylon's destruction as cataclysmic, rendering the land uninhabitable. But consider:

> When Cyrus personally entered Babylon he was welcomed by the populace. He proclaimed peace to everyone in the city. The temples functioned as usual and care was taken to make the transition to Persian rule as painless as possible. Gobryas was made satrap of the new province of Babirush (i.e. Babylon) and many of the former officials of government were kept at their posts. A citizen of Babylon would have been unaware of the fact that a new era of history had begun.[2]

Second, these prophetic passages do not correlate with the fall of "mystery Babylon" found in Revelation 17. The appellation "mystery" indicates that the author is presenting a deeper, symbolic thought—one other than a mere physical location. Revelation 17 is instead referring to the Babylonian/Roman religion. Conversely, Jeremiah 50 tells us that Jeremiah is speaking about the physical location, "Babylon, the land of the Chaldeans"—modern Iraq.

A Nation Ripe for Judgment

Jeremiah and Isaiah depict Babylon as a nation ripe for judgment. She has derived pleasure from oppressing Israel. God Himself directs her destruction, assuming it as His personal "work." He "sets a snare" to bring her to judgment, intending to exact vengeance for His temple and His people. A "great nation and many kings" are "aroused from the remote parts of the earth" to execute His judgment. Turkey and Iran are subsequently called to battle. Jacob, God's "weapon of war," wreaks his vengeance for evil committed by Babylon against Israel. Babylon is skillfully destroyed and is henceforth a perpetual desolation. The land can "never again be inhabited or dwelt in from generation to generation."

It is still too early in the unfolding of Middle East events to definitively state whether or not we have been witnessing the final judgment of Babylon. But there are striking similarities between what has transpired and the prophecies of Jeremiah and Isaiah. Only the complete fulfillment of these passages can assure us that we have made a "positive ID" of a prophetic fulfillment.

However, in Jeremiah 50:18,19, the prophet may have given us a "date stamp" for Babylon's destruction—the time of Israel's rebirth and her territorial expansion. The territorial expansion specifically mentioned in this passage includes biblical Bashan (the Golan Heights), Ephraim (the West Bank), and Gilead (Jordan's East Bank).

America in Prophecy?

For those who have been desperately looking for the United States in Bible prophecy, the Gulf War and its sequel could be it.

First, the United States probably has more believing Christians per capita than any other nation on earth. Perhaps these are God's "consecrated ones" mentioned by Jeremiah. It is interesting to note that there are many practicing Christians in the armed forces. The Saudis were shocked that these supposed "infidels" from the West actually worship God. Second, the prophets describe a "great nation" that is remotely located relative to Iraq. That is a reasonably good description of the

United States, which lies oceans away. The January 20, 1991, *New York Times* indicated that Hussein "knew the Americans were over the horizon and believed they were not about to budge." If the Gulf War truly is the beginning of the fulfillment of Jeremiah's and Isaiah's prophecies, then the great nation described here is the U.S.A.:

> Behold, a people is coming from the north, and a great nation and many kings will be aroused from the remote parts of the earth (Jeremiah 50:41).

> I have commanded My consecrated ones, I have even called My mighty warriors, My proudly exulting ones, to execute My anger. A sound of tumult on the mountains, like that of many people! A sound of the uproar of kingdoms, of nations gathering together! The Lord of hosts is mustering the army for battle. They are coming from a far country from the farthest horizons, the Lord and His instruments of indignation, to destroy the whole land (Isaiah 13:3-5).

The Multi-Year War

Certainly the brief Gulf War did not eliminate Hussein or his grand ambitions. The Gulf War may yet have a second phase. Jeremiah seems to indicate the destruction of Babylon would span more than one year:

> Now lest your heart grow faint, and you be afraid at the report that will be heard in the land—for the report will come one year, and after that another report in another year,

and violence will be in the land with ruler
against ruler (Jeremiah 51:46).

Global Terrorism

Iraq's terror has not been limited to her own neighborhood. This nation threatened innocent lives worldwide, and her violence was not limited to human life.
She authored "eco-terrorism." Not only has Iraq fouled
the Persian Gulf with crude oil, but she also set fire to
some 600 Kuwaiti oil fields before withdrawing from
Kuwait. Jeremiah calls her the "hammer of the whole
earth":

> The noise of battle is in the land, and great
> destruction. How the hammer of the whole
> earth has been cut off and broken! How Baby-
> lon has become an object of horror among the
> nations! (Jeremiah 50:22,23).

Success in the Air

The war was successful due to its initial air campaign. Jeremiah gives us a literary picture of a modern
air campaign using archaic language. As one might
expect, a modern air campaign described 2500 years
ago would include the terminology of the air assault
weapons of that day—"bows," "arrows," and "javelins":

> Summon many against Babylon, all those who
> bend the bow: Encamp against her on every
> side, let there be no escape (Jeremiah 50:29).

> Behold, a people is coming from the north, and
> a great nation and many kings will be aroused
> from the remote parts of the earth. They seize

their bow and javelin; they are cruel and have
no mercy (Jeremiah 50:41,42).

The allied forces sometimes flew in excess of 2000
sorties a day. These have been described as "wave after
wave" of assault. "Waves" are part of the word picture
used by God's prophet to describe the buffeting of Babylon:

How Babylon has become an object of horror
among the nations! The sea has come up over
Babylon; she has been engulfed with its tu-
multuous waves. Her cities have become an
object of horror, a parched land and a desert, a
land in which no man lives, and through which
no son of man passes (Jeremiah 51:41-43).

And consider this word picture of swarming aircraft:

I will fill you with a population like locusts,
and they will cry out with shouts of victory
over you (Jeremiah 51:14).

The bombing was liberally applied. The words frequently used in military briefings to describe this are
"saturation bombing." The destroyers of Babylon are
also instructed in Jeremiah to be liberal:

Shoot at her, do not be sparing with your
arrows, for she has sinned against the Lord
(Jeremiah 50:14).

The bombing of Iraq was carried out with surgical
precision. Peter Arnett of CNN reported during the first
night of bombing in Baghdad, "Every bomb seems to be
hitting something." His colleague, Bernard Shaw of
CNN, reported, "We are seeing surgical bombing. No

bombs out of pattern." Jeremiah describes this precision as well:

> Their arrows will be like an expert warrior who does not return empty-handed (Jeremiah 50:9).

The January 19, 1991, *New York Times* reported: "Baghdad is suffering from a complete cutoff of electricity and telephone service and a severe shortage of water. Relentless explosions sent thousands of civilians fleeing for the countryside and other cities." An Iraqi correspondent for Reuters said the city was "a ghost town," and described terrified civilians "who pray for the safety of their families as bombs shake homes and rattle windows." Unlike the first fall of Babylon, Jeremiah describes the utter desolation of Babylon's cities:

> Her cities have become an object of horror, a parched land and a desert, a land in which no man lives, and through which no son of man passes (Jeremiah 51:43).

Iraqi Hostility Toward Israel

Hussein, a secularist, turned the Gulf War into a war against the God of Israel. He called all Moslems to rise up in a holy war and liberate Palestine from the "infidels." He set himself in direct opposition to God's work of regathering of the nation of Israel. Is there any wonder that God will judge him and his nation?

> Repay her according to her work; according to all that she has done, so do to her; for she has become arrogant against the Lord, against the Holy One of Israel (Jeremiah 50:29).

During the Gulf War, Israel came under heavy assault from Iraqi SCUD missiles. While this was happening, a few Jews fled Israel to escape the bombing and pacify their nervous relatives; but many more flew to Israel to join her in her hour of need. One group of Orthodox Jews organized "Operation Torah Shield" to petition God for Israel's protection. The miraculous protection that Israel enjoyed would indicate that their operation was successful.

> They will ask for the way to Zion, turning their faces in its direction; they will come that they may join themselves to the Lord in an everlasting covenant that will not be forgotten (Jeremiah 50:5).

Healing the Mortal Wounds?

Looking to the end of the war, George Bush said, "When all this is over we want to be healers."[3] By that he probably meant sending in U.S. contractors to help rebuild Iraq after declaring victory and then leaving quickly. Unfortunately, at the end of the ground war Iraq began "hemorrhaging" refugees. Hundreds of thousands of Kurds and Shiite Moslems fled to the borders seeking asylum from the still-intact Hussein regime. Bush was thus pressured to stay longer than planned and apply a tourniquet. But unlike his unequivocal support for providing Israeli land for the "homeless Palestinians," Bush has no intention of advocating snatching a piece of Arab land for the homeless, non-Arab Kurds. Jeremiah also foresaw the futile and halfhearted efforts of the nations to heal Babylon:

> Bring balm for her pain; perhaps she may be healed. We applied healing to Babylon, but she was not healed; forsake her and let us each go to his own country, for her judgment has reached to heaven and towers up to the very skies (Jeremiah 51:8,9).

Intervention by Surrounding Nations

After the land of Babylon has been beaten down or "winnowed" (Jeremiah 51:2), and the coalition forces have half-heartedly tried to heal Babylon and gone home (Jeremiah 51:8,9), then Phase II of the Gulf War may begin. Jeremiah has prophesied that the "Medes" and the kings of "Ararat, Minni, and Ashkenaz" would participate in Babylon's fall (Jeremiah 51:27,28).

Ararat, Minni, and Ashkenaz were areas now located in western Turkey. A recent *New York Times* editorial (May 2, 1991) noted that some scholars believe the Kurds are descended from the Medes. The Medes occupied an area which is now in northern Iran. Therefore, Jeremiah could be speaking about the Iranians or the Kurds. These peoples did not play a significant role in the air or ground war, but they have been active in post-war rebellions and may yet play a major role in Phase II.

Even before the Gulf War ended, analysts were predicting that a weakened or destroyed Iraq might face dismemberment at the hands of her neighbors. Turkey, Iran, and Syria politically and militarily positioned themselves for such a move. Each distrusts the motives of the others and is ready to pounce if it thinks another nation will beat it to the punch. If Iran does make a major military move, Turkey and Syria would be pressured to respond in kind to protect their own interests and borders.

The Gulf War— After the Intermission

So here's the 64,000-dollar question:

> Is the Gulf War truly over and we have not been witnessing the fulfillment of the prophetic judgment of Babylon, or are we merely between battles?

If the judgment of Babylon is a distant future event, then we will not see Jeremiah 50 and 51 and Isaiah 13 fulfilled to the letter at this time. To date these passages have not been completely fulfilled. However, this may be merely an intermission. We must not be in a rush when evaluating the long-term affairs of nations. In Jeremiah 51 we find the following passage which appears to indicate that there could be a pause between the "pounding" of Iraq and the "harvest" of her judgment.

> Thus says the Lord of hosts, the God of Israel: "The daughter of Babylon is like a threshing floor at the time it is stamped firm; yet in a little while the time of harvest will come for her" (Jeremiah 51:33).

However, if we are merely at an intermission, what can we expect to see in the near future?

Retaliation by Israel

Modern Israel has a military heart. Israel by definition means "soldier of God." Ezekiel tells us that when God regathers Israel, just as He is doing in our day, Israel will be raised from the grave as "an exceedingly great army."[4] Jeremiah indicates that Israel, this great military power, will play a key role in God's judgment of Babylon. During the Gulf War, Israel was passive and silent. Therefore we may yet see a fulfillment of this prophecy in Phase II of the Gulf War:

> The portion of Jacob is not like these; for the Maker of all is He, and of the tribe of His inheritance; the Lord of hosts is His name. He says, "You are My war-club, My weapon of war; and with you I shatter nations, and with you I destroy kingdoms, and with you I shatter the

the horse and his rider, and with you I shatter
the chariot and its rider, and with you I shatter man and woman, and with you I shatter old
man and youth, and with you I shatter young
man and virgin, and with you I shatter the
shepherd and his flock, and with you I shatter
the farmer and his team, and with you I shatter governors and prefects. But I will repay
Babylon and all the inhabitants of Chaldea for
all their evil that they have done in Zion before
your eyes," declares the Lord (Jeremiah 51:19-
24).

During the Gulf War, Israel showed great, uncharac-
teristic restraint by not responding to repeated Iraqi
missile attacks. One of the major reasons for this was to
curry favor with the United States and Europe. She
knew she would need this goodwill "on account" in the
postwar period when efforts would be made to negotiate
a Middle East Peace Covenant. Unfortunately, Western
memories are very short, and Israel cooperation has
nearly faded from memory.

Many in Israel fear that their restraint has been
viewed as a sign of weakness, and long for an excuse to
retaliate. If the Israelis find that opportunity, their blow
will be devastating. The *New York Times* reported on
January 24, 1991, the four criteria for an Israeli assault,
the last point being that ". . . any Israeli attack on Iraq
would have to leave 'painful scars that would stay with
them for a long time.' " Decisive and devastating Israeli
participation in the Gulf War may be planned for Phase II.

The End of Iraq

Whether or not there is a Phase II to the Gulf War, the
prophets are explicit about the final state of Iraq: It will
be a perpetual devastation. Even as a result of Phase I,

"A United Nations survey of civilian damage caused by the allied bombardment of Iraq calls the results 'near apocalyptic'... the bombing has relegated Iraq 'to a pre-industrial age'..."[5] But God is not finished with her. Whether through nuclear, biological, chemical, or conventional forces, Iraq will become uninhabitable and Hussein's palace will have interesting new occupants.

> Thou, O Lord, hast promised concerning this place [Babylon] to cut it off, so that there will be nothing dwelling in it, whether man or beast, but it will be a perpetual desolation (Jeremiah 51:62).

> Therefore the desert creatures will live there along with the jackals; the ostriches also will live in it, and it will never again be inhabited or dwelt in from generation to generation. As when God overthrew Sodom and Gomorrah with its neighbors," declares the Lord, "No man will live there, nor will any son of man reside in it" (Jeremiah 50:39,40).

> Babylon, the beauty of kingdoms, the glory of the Chaldeans' pride, will be as when God overthrew Sodom and Gomorrah. It will never be inhabited or lived in from generation to generation; nor will the Arab pitch his tent there, nor will shepherds make their flocks lie down there. But desert creatures will lie down there, and their houses will be full of owls, ostriches also will live there, and shaggy goats will frolic there. And hyenas will howl in their fortified towers and jackals in their luxurious palaces (Isaiah 13:19-22).

While this devastation could be caused by nuclear, chemical, or biological weapons, it could also be the result of Hussein's own eco-terrorism. The burning oil fields in Kuwait coated and destroyed plant life, threatened Persian Gulf sea life, and blackened the lungs of wildlife. One report indicated that the burning of the Kuwaiti oil fields could cause even longer-term devastation.

Black rain from the burning oil wells of Kuwait is expected to fall up to 2,000 kilometers away in parts of Eastern Europe and poison the Gulf region for at least a decade.... The highly acidic rain is likely to contaminate public water supplies and damage the fragile, semi-arid agricultural economy in parts of Iran and the Middle East.... Professor Kalheinz Balchniter, of Ulm University's Institute for Agricultural and Environmental Chemistry, said, "What is happening in the Gulf is like a terrible chemical experiment never witnessed before. The best we can hope is that we may learn from it." The German scientist believes that the best agricultural regions in the Gulf will have to be decontaminated by special earth-burning and washing techniques. Professor Balchniter added: "There is little rain in the desert. The chemical and biological process that would lead to the pollution being naturally dispersed in Europe work far more slowly in the desert." Hydrocarbons in the black rain could cause cancer and are likely to be consumed and drunk by humans, fish and livestock in the affected regions, which could include the Caspian region of the Soviet Union as well as parts of the Balkans already suffering chronic pollution problems. Worst affected, however, will be Iran and, ironically, Iraq. The director of research at Britain's Meteorological Office, Keith Browning, said: "... The burning wells are going to keep pumping out smoke and acid rain in the same region of the world and that is bad. The only good thing is that it will not be a continual accumulation in the atmosphere. The rain will wash it out." If the rain pollutes underground water sources essential for life in the harsh desert environment, some areas could be rendered uninhabitable. Robert Boucher, a pollution expert with the Paris-based 'Amis de la Terre' (Friends of the Earth), said: "It could take 50 years for those sources to clean up."[6]

In any case, two things are now clear. First, Iraq will be judged by God for her treatment of Israel and her arrogance to the God of Israel. If that judgment is not now in progress, it will surely occur in the future. Second, the conduct of the Gulf War has established a battle plan for Armageddon. A single nation has been declared an outlaw and condemned by the ruling "world government." As a result of this condemnation, a call to battle was authorized. The peoples of the world responded to that call and encircled that nation, intent on her destruction. In 1991 the object of the world's judgment was Iraq. In the not-too-distant future the nation being encircled will be Israel, and Armageddon will begin!

The Fall of the King

Saddam Hussein sees himself as a glorious king of Babylon. The fourteenth chapter of Isaiah gives us a detailed picture of the demise of a Babylonian ruler. Is it possible that the ruler being described is Saddam Hussein? Again, there is strong circumstantial evidence that it is, but only time will tell. We are provided with a "date stamp" for this prophecy in the first verses of this chapter. The fall of this king will occur after Israel is "again" settled in her land. Could this refer to an unspecified period after 1948 when Israel regained her sovereignty after some 2500 years of occupation that began with Babylon?

> When the Lord will have compassion on Jacob,
> and again choose Israel, and settle them in
> their own land.... And it will be in the day
> when the Lord gives you rest from your pain
> and turmoil and harsh service in which you
> have been enslaved that you will take up this
> taunt against the king of Babylon...[7]

Isaiah describes the details of the King of Babylon's
fall. Is this the fall of Saddam Hussein?

- ♦ This ruler has been striking "the peoples in fury
  with unceasing strokes, which subdued the nations in anger with unrestrained persecution"
  (Isaiah 14:6). Consider Hussein's eight-year war
  with Iran, immediately followed by his annexation of Kuwait and his frustrated attempt to
  invade Saudi Arabia. Also consider his gassing of
  the Kurds, his oppression of the Shiite Moslems,
  and his bombing of Israel.

- ♦ He has disquieted the entire world. It is asked,
  "Is this the man who made the earth tremble,
  who shook the kingdoms?" (v. 16). He has "weakened the nations" (v. 12). At his fall, "The whole
  earth is at rest and is quiet; they break forth into
  shouts of joy" (v. 7). Hussein has invaded some
  nations, attacked others, threatened worldwide
  terrorism, caused political division in most nations as they discussed response to his aggres-
  sion, and caused widespread economic instability
  and debt. His passing would certainly be cause
  for relief.

- ♦ He has lived opulently, acquiring rare foreign
  woods: "Even the cypress trees rejoice over you,
  and the cedars of Lebanon, saying, 'Since you
  were laid low, no tree cutter comes up against

us.'" (v. 8). His "pomp and the music" of his harps are gone (v. 11). Hussein has built for himself numerous opulent palaces and a network of elaborate security bunkers.

• He has wielded great power, for dead kings greet him saying, "Even you have been made weak as we..." (v. 10). Hussein led one of the largest armies in the world.

• He has had divine ambitions (v. 13). Hussein is a cultic figure. "Saddam's photo hangs in most schools, businesses, homes and taxis here, even bathrooms. His face is on buttons and watches; children have changed the traditional Muslim greeting of 'Salaamu Alaikum,' 'peace be unto you,' to 'Saddam Alaikum': Peace be unto Saddam.... The late Arab intellectual and politician Michel Aflaq summed up Saddam's importance to Arabs in one of his last speeches: 'Saddam is God's gift to Iraq and the Iraqi gift to the Arab nation.'"[8]

• He has been an eco-terrorist, and "made the world like a wilderness" (v. 17). Hussein caused an oil spill in the Persian Gulf which caused widespread destruction of wildlife. He also set fire to over 600 Kuwaiti oil wells, which are polluting the air, the ground surface, and the aquifers.

• He conquered cities and took hostages (v. 17). Hussein captured many cities, the most prominent of which was Kuwait City. Before the Gulf War started, Hussein implemented the practice of using his Western "guests" as human shields at strategic sites. During the conduct of the war he not only took military prisoners of war, but he took large portions of the Kuwaiti population hostage.

- ◆ He is responsible for ruining his country and slaying his own people (v. 20). Can any less be said of Hussein?

- ◆ He is so hated that he is not given a state burial, but lies in a mass grave as a "trampled corpse" (v. 19).

- ◆ His sons are executed to ensure that they will not follow in his footsteps (v. 21).

I believe that Isaiah 14 provides us with a near-perfect description of Saddam Hussein's life and times to date. The only inconsistencies are those which may yet be fulfilled. If Hussein ends up in a mass grave, and his sons are executed, the picture will be complete and our identification confirmed.

The Judgment of Jordan and Arabia

Modern Jordan became an independent state in 1946. In 1948, her armies seized the West Bank and East Jerusalem from Israel. When Jordan's King Abdullah negotiated a truce with Israel, he was promptly assassinated. He was succeeded by his grandson, King Hussein. Jordan has participated unsuccessfully in many Arab-Israeli wars—most notably its loss of the "stolen" West Bank and East Jerusalem in 1967.

The hostility between Jordan and Israel has ancient roots. The nation of Jordan is comprised of three ancient tribes: Moab, Ammon, and Edom. Moabites and Ammonites are the descendants of Lot by his incestuous daughters, and Edomites are the descendants of Esau, Jacob's twin brother.

These nations have always been at odds with the children of Israel. God will ultimately punish Jordan for its treatment of Israel. In fact, numerous prophecies tell us that Israel will ultimately possess Jordan. Today, just the opposite is true. Jordan occupies the East Bank of the Jordan River, which is the inheritance of Israel's son, Gad. This is a fulfillment of prophecy:

> Concerning the sons of Ammon. Thus says the Lord: "Does Israel have no sons? Or has he no heirs? Why then has Malcam [the national god of the Ammonites] taken possession of Gad and his people settled in its cities? Therefore, behold, the days are coming," declares the Lord, "that I shall cause a trumpet blast of war to be heard against Rabbah of the sons of Ammon; and it will become a desolate heap, and her towns will be set on fire. Then Israel will take possession of his possessors," says the Lord (Jeremiah 49:1,2).

This Israeli territorial expansion is echoed in the prophecies of Obadiah. In fact the main theme of Obadiah is the destruction of Edom, which lies in southern Jordan:

> "Then the house of Jacob will be a fire and the house of Joseph a flame; but the house of Esau [Edom] will be as stubble. And they will set them on fire and consume them, so that there will be no survivor of the house of Esau," for the Lord has spoken. Then those of the Negev [southern Israel] will possess the mountain of Esau, and those of the Shephelah [Judean hills near Gaza] the Philistine plain [Gaza]; also, they will possess the territory of Ephraim and the territory of Samaria [West Bank], and Benjamin will possess Gilead [East Bank] (Obadiah 18,19).

When Will Israel Possess Jordan?

It is difficult to determine when Israel will possess Jordan relative to other prophetic events, but we are provided with some clues. It seems that there are two plausible times—during the battle of Armageddon, or during the judgment of Babylon.

In the passage from Obadiah 18 and 19, Jacob and Joseph are described as "fires" and "flames" when they possess Edom. In the description of Armageddon provided in Zechariah 12:4-9, Judah is described as a "firepot" consuming all of her neighbors. Perhaps this common simile used in describing Israel indicates that the possession described in Obadiah will occur at Armageddon:

> In that day I will make the clans of Judah like a firepot among pieces of wood and a flaming torch among sheaves, so they will consume on the right hand and on the left all the surrounding peoples, while the inhabitants of Jerusalem again dwell on their own sites in Jerusalem (Zechariah 12:6).

Alternatively Israel may possess Jordan sooner than the battle of Armageddon. First, it is clear from Isaiah 11 that the possession will occur at the time of the "second regathering of Israel," that is, sometime after 1948:

> Then it will happen on that day that the Lord will again recover the second time with His hand the remnant of His people, who will remain, from Assyria, Egypt, Pathros, Cush, Elam, Shinar, Hamath, and from the islands [coastlands] of the sea. And He will lift up a standard for the nations, and will assemble

the banished ones of Israel, and will gather the dispersed of Judah from the four corners of the earth. . . . And they will swoop down on the slopes of the Philistines on the west [Gaza]; together they will plunder the sons of the east; they will possess Edom and Moab; and the sons of Ammon will be subject to them (Isaiah 11:11,12,14).

We are told in Zephaniah 2:8-11 that Ammon and Moab will be destroyed as Sodom and Gomorrah, plundered by Israel and possessed. In Jeremiah 49:17-19, we are told that Edom will also be destroyed as Sodom and Gomorrah. It is interesting that the description of the fall of Edom is incredibly similar to that of Babylon. We know that Israel will be used to judge the three tribes of Jordan, and we also know that Israel is the Lord's "war-club," which He wields against Babylon. In that Edom and Babylon have a common destroyer, and meet a common fate, perhaps the timing of their destructions is coincident.

EDOM	BABYLON
Jeremiah 49:17	*Jeremiah 50:13*
And Edom will become an object of horror; everyone who passes by it will be horrified and will hiss at all its wounds.	Everyone who passes by Babylon will be horrified and will hiss because of all her wounds.
49:18	*50:40*
"Like the overthrow of Sodom and Gomorrah with its neighbors," says the Lord,	"As when God overthrew Sodom and Gomorrah with its neighbors," declares the Lord, "no man will live there,

"no one will live there, nor will a son of man reside in it."

49:19
Behold, one will come up like a lion from the thickets of the Jordan against a perennially watered pasture; for in an instant I shall make him run away from it, and whoever is chosen I shall appoint over it. For who is like Me, and who will summon Me into court? And who then is the shepherd who can stand against Me?

nor will any son of man reside in it."

50:44
Behold, one will come up like a lion from the thicket of the Jordan to a perennially watered pasture; for in an instant I shall make them run away from it, and whoever is chosen I shall appoint over it. For who is like Me, and who will summon Me into court? And who then is the shepherd who can stand against Me?

The possession of Edom is associated with the repairing of the tabernacle. We know that Israel will be sacrificing to God during the first half of the seven-year Middle East Peace Covenant. Could it be that they will both possess Edom and repair the tabernacle immediately before or after the signing of the Middle East Peace Covenant?

"In that day I will raise up the fallen booth of David, and wall up its breaches; I will also raise up its ruins, and rebuild it as in the days of old; that they may possess the remnant of Edom and all the nations who are called by My name," declares the Lord who does this (Amos 9:11,12).

A Scenario: If Jordan is Possessed When Babylon Is Judged

As we have discussed, the day may soon come in Phase II of the Gulf War when Israel retaliates against Iraq. Such a venture would almost certainly require violation of Jordanian airspace. During the early days of the Gulf War, the Jordanian government declared that such an incursion would be considered an act of war. Therefore, should Israel exercise its right to retaliate, an Israeli-Jordanian war is almost assured.

If an Israeli-Jordanian war does take place, Jordan will be vanquished and probably with lightning speed. In a previous war, it took Israel a mere two hours to eliminate the Jordanian airforce. After such a war, Israel will then occupy the East Bank. Will we soon witness another major land grant to Israel from her Lord? The prophets tell us that this must happen; it is the timing and prophetic sequence that is "fuzzy."

Prophetic Possibilities

If Phase II of the Gulf War precipitates Israel's possession of Jordan, it could open some very interesting prophetic possibilities!

First, Israel would end up with a comfortable "security zone." Her territorial borders would be greatly expanded. She would then be in possession of the complete territory promised to her by Britain in the Balfour Declaration. To the east, her large and powerful enemy, Iraq, would be totally destroyed.

Israel's tiny size and continuous oppression has produced a well-deserved state of paranoia. This paranoia is considered to be the root of many Middle East peace failures. Therefore, if Israel is put at ease by this "security zone," she may let her guard down and allow herself to be persuaded to sign the Middle East Peace Covenant. This expanded territory may give her the confidence that she needs to willingly divide her land in exchange for peace. It is this division of "God's land" that is one of God's motives for gathering the nations at Armageddon.[9] This "security zone" could also be part of the reason that Israel is described as enjoying a period of peace at the onset of the Russo-Israeli War.

Second, during the evil prince's reign in Jerusalem, Israel will be brutally oppressed. In Matthew 24:16, Jesus counsels his brothers: "Let those who are in Judea flee to the mountains." Some scholars believe that Israel will flee into the Jordanian mountains. This would be more feasible if Israel possessed Jordan.

Third, the possession of Jordan could play an active part in restoring temple worship in Israel! For almost two millennia Israel has not had a proper temple, or a priesthood that could perform the rituals ordained in the law. This could soon change!

The Amos 9:11,12 passage previously noted describes the restoration of the tabernacle. It is interesting that this same prophecy also mentions the possession of the portion of Jordan called Edom. In this prophetic reference from Amos, it sounds as if God is going to "resurrect" David's tabernacle. How does this relate to Israel's possession of Jordan?

There is a mountain in Jordan called Nebo. The original tabernacle, the ark of the covenant and the altar of incense may have been hidden by Jeremiah on Mount Nebo prior to the Babylonian looting of the temple. This event is described in the apocryphal book of 2 Maccabees. Although the books of the Apocrypha are not part of the Jewish or Christian canon, they do provide valuable historical information. Second Maccabees 2:1-8 tells us that the exact location of the original tabernacle, the ark of the covenant, and the altar of incense on Mount Nebo would be hidden until the "gathering of the congregation of his people." Again, God's regathering of

His people in the land of Israel is the "date stamp" for this significant reference.

If Israel possesses Jordan, it could result in the return of the lost tabernacle and temple treasures to Jerusalem after 2500 years! Would it not be just like our God to restore Israel's temple treasures using His judgment of their original oppressor, Babylon? Would it not be just like our God to restore temple worship using an act of judgment which He describes as "vengeance for His temple" (Jeremiah 50:28; 51:11)?

If God chooses this time to restore the tabernacle, the ark of the covenant and the altar of incense to Israel, perhaps other treasures will be restored as well. One of these treasures is the "kalal" containing the ashes of the red heifer.

The kalal is a pot which contains the ashes of a sacrifice described in Numbers 19. These ashes are required for the purification of individuals, especially the priesthood. When Jerusalem was under siege by the Romans in 70 A.D., the kalal and other treasures were hidden in the Judean hills. Israel cannot resume biblical temple worship until these ashes are found and the priesthood is purified.

Two searches are currently underway. Some members of the Jewish community are not waiting for the original ashes to be discovered. They are making a worldwide search for a spotless red heifer. A second search is underway for the ancient kalal, believed to be located in the caves of Qumran. In 1989, these excavations produced a small vessel of rare, 2,000-year-old balsam oil. Hopefully, these digs will soon produce the kalal.

A detailed description of this search for these ashes and their significance may be found in *The Next Move: Current Events in Bible Prophecy* by Rob Lindsted. Dr. Lindsted also points out the significance of these ashes to the entire nation of Islam. He writes:

Finding the ashes of the red heifer is important even to the Arabs. The Moslem bible is
the Koran, and the first book is called Parah,
which literally translated means "The Calf."
The Moslems believe that whoever finds the
ashes will rule the world. That's why the Arab
countries are just as interested as the Jews in
finding the little kalal containing the ashes of
the last red heifer.[10]

If Israel finds the kalal, it is interesting to consider
what effect it might have on the Moslem world. Will
Moslems be obedient to their faith and cease to oppress
Israel? Will this add to Israel's "security zone"?

Arabia in Prophecy

In Isaiah 21 we have a prophecy of the fall of Arabia. It
is very difficult to determine whether this has been
historically fulfilled or whether we will yet see the fall of
Saudi Arabia. The chapter begins by addressing the
defeat of Babylon at the hands of Iran (Media and Elam).
This may indicate that Arabia will fall subsequent to
Phase II of the Gulf War. The chapter then describes
how fugitives from the fighting will flee to Arabia and
must be met with water and bread. The chapter closes
by saying:

> For thus the Lord said to me, "In a year, as a
> hired man would count it, all the splendor of
> Kedar [Arabia] will terminate; and the re-
> mainder of the number of bowmen, the mighty
> men of the sons of Kedar, will be few; for the
> Lord God of Israel has spoken" (Isaiah 21:16,17).

Thus it appears that Arabia will cease to be a pros-
perous, mighty nation exactly a year after the influx of
fugitives from Babylon's fall. We know that it is "exactly

a year" because of the expression "a year as a hired man would count it." A hired man wants a strict accounting of his time. He does not want the term of his employment shortened, thus cutting his wages, nor does he want the terms of his employment lengthened to his disadvantage, thus adding to his labor. If we see an Iranian military move against Iraq, we should keep an eye on Saudi Arabia! It seems possible that the primary reason Saudi Arabia will not be involved in the Russo-Israeli War is that they do not have the means or the ability to do so.

The Future of Egypt and Assyria

Although Israel and Egypt have historically had their differences, Egypt is the only Moslem nation which is not formally in a state of war with Israel. As a result of the 1979 Camp David Accords, Israel and Egypt are officially at peace. As a direct result of signing this treaty, Egypt was ostracized from the Arab camp for ten years. Although this peace with Israel did not please her Moslem brothers, it is clear that it has pleased Israel's God. It appears that Egypt's bravery on the spiritual battleground may have earned her a special place in the messianic kingdom.

In Isaiah 19 we have a prophecy about Egypt and "Assyria." While we can all easily identify Egypt on a map, "Assyria" is more difficult. The Assyrians originally lived in an area which is now the much-contested and mythical "Kurdistan." Their empire eventually covered the entire "Fertile Crescent"—the Tigris-Euphrates Valley and the eastern Mediterranean coastline. While the original inhabitants near the northeast Mediterranean coast were called Arameans (sons of Aram), that area soon became known as "Syria," from the name "Assyria." Therefore, in determining the modern identity of

Assyria, we can each draw our own conclusions. However, in that modern Syria began discussing "land for peace" with Israel before the Gulf War began, perhaps it is Syria who will also earn a special place in the messianic kingdom. In any case, God surely knows the peoples with whom He is dealing, and we will be able to identify them as prophecy is fulfilled.

This passage has no clear "date stamp," so it is difficult to determine whether this has been historically fulfilled or is yet in our future. I believe that this could be a futuristic prophecy because of the final state in which we find Egypt and Assyria. This description has a distinctive messianic kingdom ring to it!

Here is an outline of the events of Isaiah 19:

- Egypt is convulsed by a civil war (v. 2). Could this be the result of factionalism caused by the Gulf War?

- Egypt is given into the hands of "a cruel master" and "a mighty king" (v. 4). Could this be the evil prince's regime and his appointed "king of the South" mentioned in Daniel 11:40?

- Egypt endures economic hardship (vv. 5-15). The Nile River dries up and there is no work.

- Egypt becomes afraid of the Lord and is terrorized by Israel and God's work there (vv. 16,17).

- Egypt has a spiritual awakening; five of its cities begin to speak Hebrew and worship God "with sacrifice and offering" (vv. 18, 19,21).

- Egypt will be sent a Savior to deliver them (v. 20). Could this be when Messiah returns and destroys the evil prince, thus delivering not only Israel but Egypt and the entire world?

♦ Egypt will be "pruned"—stricken, but with a healing blow (v. 22). Could this be referring to the judgment of the nations, where Messiah will separate His followers and dispose of His enemies?

The chapter ends with these exciting words:

> In that day there will be a highway from Egypt to Assyria, and the Assyrians will come into Egypt and the Egyptians into Assyria, and the Egyptians will worship with the Assyrians. In that day Israel will be the third party with Egypt and Assyria, a blessing in the midst of the earth, whom the Lord of hosts has blessed, saying, "Blessed is Egypt My people, and Assyria the work of My hands, and Israel My inheritance" (Isaiah 19:23-25).

We also know from Zechariah 14:16-19 that during the messianic kingdom Egypt will travel to Jerusalem to worship the King, the Lord of Hosts, and to celebrate "Succoth" (the Feast of Booths) every year. If they or any other surviving nation does not fulfill this requirement they will have no rain.

From these passages I believe we can deduce that some of Israel's immediate neighbors will have a believing remnant who will not be totally destroyed, but will become subjects in good standing in the messianic kingdom.

A Scenario for the Future

If the Gulf War has truly begun the judgment of Iraq, what might we expect in the near future? To be sure, there are numerous viable scenarios. Let's try to pull together some of these prophetic events into one such Middle Eastern scenario.

- ◆ The coalition forces leave Iraq after halfhearted attempts to "heal" her and her massive refugee problems (Jeremiah 51:9).

- ◆ Phase II of the Gulf War breaks out when the northern "security zone" established by the departed coalition forces to shelter the Kurds is attacked by the Iraqi military. This fighting so close to the Turkish and Iranian border soon expands into a full-blown war. The coalition forces, which have just left the area, are reluctant to return.

- ◆ To curry favor and support from the radical Arab/ Moslem community, Iraq may again threaten or even attack Israel through Jordan—"the Mother of all Suicides" (Jeremiah 50:44). This would result in a massive Israeli attack on Iraq (Jeremiah 51:19-24).

- ◆ An Israeli retaliatory strike could start and immediately end an Israeli–Jordanian War, leaving Israel in possession of Jordan (Isaiah 11:14). It could also perpetually devastate Iraq (Jeremiah 51:62-64).

- ◆ The strength which Israel exhibits in the destruction of Babylon may strike long-lasting terror into Moslem hearts: "The land of Judah will become a terror to Egypt" (Isaiah 19:17).

- ◆ Middle East and World attention would be focused on the dismembering of Iraq as Turkey, Iran, Kurdistan, and Syria descend on the "corpse" of Iraq.

- Some Moslem nations, especially Egypt (Isaiah 19:2) and Turkey, may be faced with civil unrest from radical factions in their populations. Radical control of the Turkish government could lead to eventual Turkish involvement in the Russo-Israeli War.

- For a brief period these power plays could divert world attention from Israel, leaving them temporarily at peace within enlarged "secure" borders. This would prepare Israel for victimization in the next steps of the scenario.

- The broad support for Saddam Hussein in Asian, African, and Arab nations could bring into question the ability of the United Nations to be a fair arbiter of international justice. As the Europe "empire" grows in strength and membership, the U.N. may begin to wane as the flagship international body.

- The pressure for a comprehensive Middle East Peace Covenant would be enormous. The conference that develops the Covenant would be convened by the Europeans and the evil prince (Daniel 9:27). They would attempt to restore an equilibrium in the Middle East, and fix borders.

- One of the terms of the Covenant may be to establish a regional, supranational security administrator. Egypt, torn by civil war, could be put under the protective wing of its regional administrator (Isaiah 19:4). This leader could eventually be considered the "king of the South" (Daniel 11:40).

- Another of the terms of this Covenant may be the division of the Temple Mount. The existing Moslem sites, the Dome of the Rock and the Aqsa

Mosque, would be protected (Revelation 11:2), and the Jews would be allowed to worship on the northern section of the platform.

♦ With permission to begin biblically ordained worship on the site of God's ancient temple, and free access to Jordan's Mount Nebo, many spiritually exciting things could begin to happen in Israel. The original tabernacle, ark of the Covenant, and altar of incense could be restored to Israel, or they may begin construction of a third temple. In either case, Torah-prescribed worship and sacrifice could become a reality after 2000 years of prayerful longing. The discovery of the ashes of the red heifer would not only purify the site of worship and the priesthood, but it could also be the death knell for Moslem-Israeli tensions.

♦ The combatants who will participate in the Ezekiel 38 and 39 Russo-Israeli war will begin to coalesce. Radical Moslem nations including Libya (Put), Sudan/Ethiopia (Cush), Iran (Persia), and Turkey (Gomer, Togarmah, Meshech, Tubal) will be jealous of the prosperity and peace which Israel has enjoyed as a result of the fall of Iraq and Jordan, and they will conspire to destroy her.

Just as significant are the moderate Moslem nations who are not listed as participants of this invasion. Saudi Arabia (Sheba and Dedan) may fall within a year of Iraq (Isaiah 21:16,17). Egypt could be under the protectorate of a regional administrator. Syria may have negotiated a peace with Israel, having begun discussions prior to the Gulf War.

♦ Russian Communist hard-liners will grow in power and author the "evil plan" to invade Israel.

Already the following sentiments are being expressed: "Some hard-line Soviet publications today questioned the Soviet Union's alliance with the U.S. against Iraq and suggested that the U.S. and Israel were aggressors as worthy of punishment as Iraq."[11] The Russians have positioned themselves in the postwar Moslem camp. Former Soviet Foreign Minister Aleksandr A. Bessmertnykh had been "cautioning the United States against destroying Iraq as the beginning of an effort by the Soviet Union to preserve its influence in the Arab world in the aftermath of the Persian Gulf war."[12]

♦ The subsequent invasion of Israel by Russia and her radical Moslem allies could create another power vacuum as God judges and destroys those nations. This one would make the post-Gulf-War power vacuum pale by comparison. With Russia, Iraq, and Libya taken out of play, this would seriously shake world political equilibrium. The European empire will seize the moment. They will move quickly to fill that void, providing a master plan for world government. This new plan will void prior covenants and give authority to the evil prince for 42 months (Revelation 13:5) to get the world under control.

♦ The battle plans for the encircling of Iraq may be dusted off and reused by the evil prince for gathering the nations to battle against Israel—a battle called Armageddon.

Although this is only one viable scenario, we have seen how easily the hostilities and maneuvering in the Middle East could lead not only to a Middle East Peace Covenant, but to Moslem/Arab involvement in the Russo-Israeli War and the eventual establishment of the European empire as a world government. As soon as the Middle East Peace Covenant is signed, the clock will begin ticking out seven years of judgment until the establishment of the messianic kingdom. The Gulf War may have set in motion the fulfillment of a wide array of end time prophetic texts.

After the Intermission

Although we now stand in the "fuzzy middle part," we will not be there for long. If events prove that we have begun to witness the fulfillment of Jeremiah's and Isaiah's prophecies, there will be many more fulfillments following quickly on their heels.

These are exciting times in which we live! The world is not spinning out of control, as many fear; God is in control.

> Let the name of God be blessed forever and ever, for wisdom and power belong to Him. And it is He who changes the times and the epochs; He removes kings and establishes kings; He gives wisdom to wise men, and knowledge to men of understanding. It is He who reveals the profound and hidden things; He knows what is in the darkness, and the light dwells with Him (Daniel 2:20-22).

God is about to judge the nations for their treatment of Israel. Pray for the world's leaders that they might realize the everlasting implications of their diplomatic decision-making. Write to your representatives in government and implore them to support the nation of Israel in any way that they can. Israel's King and Messiah is coming, and the world will soon have to answer to Him!

7

THE ISRAELI PATHWAY

The pathway of Israel is the main pathway of prophecy. It is to and through Israel that God made His promises and will fulfill them. There are two major promises:

* The Messiah

* The kingdom

First, Israel has carried the parentage of the Messiah. When God chose Abram, He promised that through him "all the families of the earth shall be blessed." The promise of that blessing is that through a son of Israel—the Messiah—reconciliation with God would be made available to all mankind.

Second, Israel is the steward of a tract of land and a city which God has reserved for Himself. The land of Israel and its capital, Jerusalem, will become the capital of the messianic kingdom. God has united His land and His people in a mystical bond. When Israel is faithful, God has assured her union with the land. When Israel has been disobedient, that bond has been broken in punishment.

The enemies of God have tried to usurp or abort the

fulfillment of these promises. This is true both historically and prophetically.

- ◆ The usurpers have posed as "antichrists." The
  English word "antichrist" is itself misleading,
  for the prefix "anti-" gives us the sense of "against."
  Actually, the literal translation means "instead
  of Christ." These usurpers have been "almost-
  Christs." History is rife with these pretenders. In
  the future the coming evil prince, apart from the
  true Messiah Himself, will appear to be the best
  hope the world has to offer. Rather than being
  totally opposite or against Messiah, he will be a
  great counterfeit.

  The usurpers have also set up "antikingdoms."
  That is to say, they have attempted to establish
  their own universal "messianic" kingdom. Again,
  history is replete with nations who have attempted
  to unify the world under their control, not the
  least of which was the Third Reich, which was
  supposed to last for a thousand years. In the
  future the evil prince will try to pull together a
  worldwide "antikingdom" of his own.

- ◆ The abortionists have repeatedly attempted to
  kill off the line of promise. This same group has
  tried to abort the rebirth of the people of Israel in
  the land of the kingdom. The history of Israel is
  the history of a people pursued by murderers.

The evil prince will be a double enemy—both usurper
and abortionist. He will temporarily usurp the role of
the Messiah and set up his global antikingdom, but
failing to gain full acceptance by Israel, he will take over
her land, sit on the throne of her God, begin killing off
all worshipers of Israel's God, call the nations to encircle

her, and attempt to defeat Israel's true Messiah in battle.

Today we see Israel's bond with her land being negotiated by some parties and openly questioned by others. Once again, her enemies are trying to separate God's people from His land. Let's look at this long history of territorial struggle.

Israel's Deed to the Land

Today the only nation whose sovereignty is seriously questioned in the world community is Israel. And yet Israel is the only nation on the face of this planet whose deed to the land sits on your bookshelf! Israel's deed to the land of Israel is found in the book of Genesis.

That book begins with the record of the creation of the universe: "In the beginning God created the heavens and the earth." Out of that vast universe, on the tiny planet called Earth, He selected a tract of land for Himself, "Eretz Yisrael"—the land of Israel. Within that land, He would select a city for Himself—Jerusalem. The Creator populated that tiny planet with a life-form modeled after Himself—mankind. From that species He chose and directed a lineage of men who would, through their progeny, fulfill His promise of a Messiah.

To one of those chosen men on this path of promise He deeded the land which He had reserved for Himself. That man was Abram, later called Abraham. In Genesis 12 God told Abram that he would carry the lineage of promise. God then commanded Abram to leave his home in Ur (modern Iraq) and to follow Him. This obedient man of faith was then led to the land of Canaan (modern Israel). Thus began the bond between the people of Israel and the land of Israel.

Once in Canaan, Abram was told that he and his descendants would possess that land. The Abrahamic family was deeded the vast tract of land from "the river of Egypt" to "the river Euphrates." When Abram asked for assurance that this would actually come to pass, we are told in Genesis 15 that God entered into a blood covenant. A blood covenant is an ancient ritual whereby those who are guaranteeing a contract cleave animals in two and then pass between the halves of the carcasses. The purpose was to visually emphasize what would happen to either guarantor if they broke the covenant. It is interesting to note that after the animals were cleft, only God passed between the carcasses. Therefore, with this act God unconditionally deeded to Abram and his descendants not only His land, but the entire "Fertile Crescent" and guaranteed it by nothing less than His own eternal life. This deed was not a shabby "99-year lease"; it was a perpetual contract. We are told in Genesis 17:7,8 that this was an "everlasting covenant" and that Canaan would be an "everlasting possession"— terms which any real estate developer would envy.

Who Owns the Land?

If the Arabs and Israelis are both descended from Abraham, who legally inherited this real-estate fortune? This question is at the heart of the Arab-Israeli conflict today, for Abraham had eight sons. His first son, Ishmael, was born to his wife's Egyptian maid. Ishmael later became the father of 12 Arab tribes. Fourteen years after the birth of Ishmael, his second son, Isaac, was born to his wife, Sarah. Isaac later became the grandfather of the 12 tribes of Israel. Abraham had six more sons by another concubine named Keturah, who later became his wife after the death of Sarah: Zimran, Jokshan, Medan, Midian, Ishbak, and Shuah.

Under Hebrew inheritance law, a firstborn son received a "double portion" or two-thirds of the father's property. Some believe that the sons of Ishmael are therefore entitled to two-thirds of Israel's land. However, by law inheritance rights applied only to the sons of *legal* wives. The sons of concubines did not participate in the division of inherited property, but were given "presents."

While the distribution of Abraham's property followed this legal formula exactly, his will did not make it to probate court. While he was still alive, he distributed his property himself. He gave all he had to his only *legal* son, Isaac.[1] He then gave gifts to his remaining seven sons and sent them away from Isaac to the land of the east. Ishmael and his sons, of whom there were 12, settled from Havilah (the Gulf Oil Emirates) to Shur (northern Sinai) "in defiance of all his relatives."[2] Thus the "Arab" branch of Abraham's family was separated from the land of Israel and the sons of Isaac. This nullifies any Arab claims to the land of Israel.

The Chosen Inheritors

God did not leave His inheritors to chance, but actively directed their selection. Even before Isaac was born, God confirmed that he would be the inheritor of God's promises and covenants.[3] Isaac later became the father of twin sons, Esau and Jacob. While they were still in the womb, God told their mother, Rebekah, that her firstborn son would serve the younger. When the two young men were grown, Esau sold his birthright to his younger brother, thus legally transferring his inheritance as firstborn to Jacob. But Isaac preferred Esau, and ignoring this "purchase," he intended to bestow upon him his full inheritance before he died. Through guile, Jacob was able to secure that which was legally his—his inheritance as firstborn and his father's blessing. Thus through Jacob, Israel's right to the land superseded the claims of Esau—father of the Edomites, one of modern Jordan's tribes.

Jacob, whose name was changed by God to "Israel," became the father of 12 sons, and thus began the 12 tribes of Israel. These 12 titleholders of Canaan were forced to flee their land holdings due to a famine. Initially they found refuge in the land of Egypt. Unfortunately, their descendants would serve the next 400 years in Egyptian slavery. However, Moses and Joshua were raised up by God, and they led the sons of Israel out of slavery and into the promised land of Canaan.

Thus from the beginning of time the land of Israel has been reserved by its Creator for Himself and His chosen inheritors. Those whom He has chosen are the sons of Israel. "Eretz Yisrael" is the eternal possession of Israel, whether they are in residence there or not. As we will see, the 400 years of Egyptian servitude was not the last time that the sons of Israel would be driven from their property.

2500 Years on the Run

When Israel has occupied her inheritance, her neighboring cousins have continuously harassed and attacked her. Twice, defeats in battle have forcibly removed Israel from the land. Both times these expulsions were punishments from her God. Perhaps this breaking of the bond between His people and His land is God's way of shaking Israel to her spiritual senses. The first expulsion was at the hands of the Babylonians, and the second was at the hands of Rome.

The Babylonian Captivity

Prior to her fall to the armies of Babylon, Israel was given one last chance to mend her ways. In Jeremiah 7 God charged Israel with:

- a prejudicial justice system
- mistreatment of the helpless
- murder of the innocent
- idolatry

Had she listened to God's faithful prophets, Israel would have been spared and would have remained united to her land:

> Amend your ways and your deeds, and I will let you dwell in this place.... For if you truly amend your ways and your deeds, if you truly practice justice between a man and his neighbor, if you do not oppress the alien, the orphan, or the widow, and do not shed innocent blood in this place, nor walk after other gods to your own ruin, then I will let you dwell in this place, in the land that I gave to your fathers forever and ever (Jeremiah 7:3,5-7).

But instead of mending her ways, Israel chose to listen to her false prophets who predicted peace. They could not believe that God would allow His own temple to be destroyed. But God preferred that His Temple be destroyed by His enemies than be defiled by His friends. Jeremiah 7 describes the nature of this defilement:

- Entire families were participating in the worship of a goddess.
- They put objects of foreign gods in the temple of the Lord.
- They set up altars to a foreign god and there sacrificed their children.

"Do you not see what they are doing in the cities of
Judah and in the streets of Jerusalem? The children gather wood, and the fathers kindle the fire,
and the women knead dough to make cakes for the
queen of heaven; and they pour out libations to
other gods in order to spite Me.... For the sons of
Judah have done that which is evil in My sight,"
declares the Lord; "they have set their detestable
things in the house which is called by My name, to
defile it. And they have built the high places of
Topheth, which is in the valley of the son of Hinnom, to burn their sons and their daughters in the
fire, which I did not command, and it did not come
into My mind. Therefore, behold, days are coming,"
declares the Lord, "when it will no more be called
Topheth, or the valley of the son of Hinnom, but the
valley of the Slaughter, for they will bury in Topheth because there is no other place. And the dead
bodies of this people will be food for the birds of the
sky, and for the beasts of the earth; and no one will
frighten them away. Then I will make to cease from
the cities of Judah and from the streets of Jerusalem the voice of joy and the voice of gladness, the
voice of the bridegroom and the voice of the bride,
for the land will become a ruin" (Jeremiah 7:17,
18,30-34).

Acting on bad advice from the false prophets in his
court, King Jehoiakim became embroiled in a war between Egypt and Babylon. His two successors continued
his doomed pro-Egyptian policies and revolted against
Babylon. By January of 588 B.C., Babylon sent its
armies into Judah to deal with this rebellious people
once and for all. For ten years Babylon had granted
Judah some degree of sovereignty and did not look
kindly upon this Judean treachery. Stronghold after

stronghold fell until Jerusalem itself was surrounded. In 587 B.C., the walls of Jerusalem were breached. On the ninth day of the Hebrew month of Av, "Tisha B'Av," the temple of God was looted and burned. The sons of Israel were carried off into captivity which would last for 70 years, just as Jeremiah had prophesied.

Israel lost its sovereignty, its temple, and its treasures, including the ark of the Covenant. After 70 years of captivity, and with the permission of King Cyrus of Medo-Persia, God regathered a remnant of Israel and His temple was rebuilt. Amazingly, much of Israel chose to remain in exile. Although Israel was once again in the land, she was no longer sovereign. Except for a brief period in the second century A.D., Israel would not regain her sovereignty until 1948 A.D., 2500 years later.

The Roman Exile

During the Roman occupation of Israel, God chose to fulfill a group of His messianic promises. In the tiny town of Beit Lechem (Bethlehem, the House of Bread), a son was born to a young Jewish maid named Miriam (Mary). She called him Yeshua (Jesus). For the next 33 years, this babe grew into a young rabbi, and He traveled the country on foot calling Israel to repentance and faith. He declared the arrival of the spiritual kingdom; the physical kingdom would come much later. Many sons of Israel accepted His message and believed that He was Messiah. Others rejected Him: Some did not want to rock the Roman boat, some did not want their own power threatened, some wanted a liberating king who would expel the Romans, rather than a spiritual redeemer.

His righteous life was ultimately sacrificed at the hands of the Roman oppressors and the corrupt Israeli leadership. What they intended for evil God intended for good. Through His substitutionary death, Messiah offered redemption to all mankind. By his life, death, and resurrection, He fulfilled a great body of prophetic messianic references. In biblical prophecy, Messiah would fulfill the roles of a suffering Servant who dies for the sins of His people, and a Redeemer/King who leads those people victoriously into the kingdom of peace. Finding it impossible to reconcile the two roles, Jewish legend and Talmudic tradition split the prophecies into two "messiahs"—Moshiach ben Yosef (Messiah son of Joseph), the suffering Servant, and Moshiach ben David (Messiah son of David), the coming King.

Messiah's arrival in Israel and call to repentance was timely. For approximately 600 years after returning from Babylonian captivity, Israel had slipped back into her old ways, and she once again faced judgment. Ezekiel 36 describes the causes of the second expulsion: spiritual impurity and idolatry, and murder of the innocent—

> Son of man, when the house of Israel was living in their own land, they defiled it by their ways and their deeds; their way before Me was like the uncleanness of a woman in her impurity. Therefore, I poured out My wrath on them for the blood which they had shed on the land, because they had defiled it with their idols. Also I scattered them among the nations, and they were dispersed throughout the lands. According to their ways and their deeds I judged them. When they came to the nations where they went, they profaned My holy name, because it was said of them, "These are the people of the Lord; yet they have come out of His land (Ezekiel 36:17-20).

Prior to the exile, Rome's domination of Israel was oppressive. All other conquered nations did not have a problem worshiping the Emperor of Rome, but Israel could not. While Israel was not faithful enough to God to please Him, she was not pagan enough to suit Rome and was therefore oppressed. In 66 A.D. Israel began to revolt. When the revolt could not be controlled by the local governor, three Roman legions were dispatched. In the year 70 A.D. Jerusalem fell, and again on the ninth day of the Hebrew month of Av, "Tisha B'Av," the temple of God was looted and burned.

This destruction of the temple was predicted by Jesus approximately 40 years earlier:

> Jesus came out from the temple and was going away when His disciples came up to point out the temple buildings to Him. And He answered and said to them, "Do you not see all these things? Truly I say to you, not one stone here shall be left upon another, which will not be torn down (Matthew 24:1,2).

The temple was made of limestone. When placed next to an accelerant, limestone crumbles, and when it is laden with water, it explodes—an awesome scene to be sure. Perhaps this is what Josephus was describing when he wrote:

> While the holy house was on fire, everything was plundered that came to hand, and ten thousand of those that were caught were slain. ... The flame was also carried a long way, and made an echo, together with the groans of those that were slain; and because this hill was high, and the works at the temple were very great, one would have thought the whole city had been on fire. Nor can one imagine anything either greater or more terrible than this noise. ... Perea did also return the echo,

as well as the mountains around about [the city], and augmented the force of the entire noise.[4]

As the temple burned, it is said that the gold ornamentation liquefied and ran between the foundation stones. The Roman soldiers, anxious to retrieve this treasure, began pulling down even the retaining walls of the temple platform. Thus Jesus' prophecy that "not one stone would be left standing upon another" was fulfilled. Today visitors to the southern wall of the Temple Mount can see the lone surviving course of the original temple wall.

With the city and the temple destroyed, Israel was scattered throughout the Roman Empire:

> It took a month for Titus to wipe out all pockets of Jewish resistance. Then, like Nebuchadnezzar, he decreed that the survivors be sent into exile, and most of Jerusalem was reduced to rubble. In all, according to Josephus, 110,000 people died by fire or famine or sword in the long campaign and siege; another 97,000 were made slaves and scattered throughout the empire.... In Jewish history, this is a turning point. It is the point from which the dominant theme of Jewish life is the diaspora, the condition of being dispersed, of being scattered.[5]

This relatively unremarkable conquest of Judea was greatly celebrated by Rome. Why would an empire which had conquered all the known peoples of the world find such delight in their conquest of the tiny and remote land of Judea? This question was raised by Abba Eban:

> There was nothing unique about the suppression of the Jewish revolt by the Romans. There

are records of revolts in Armenia, in Britain, and a particularly brutal subjection of the Belgian tribes. And yet the defeat of the Jews seems to have inspired a particular pride in the Roman commander Titus and his father, the Emperor Vespasian. Why else would they have had coins struck bearing the inscription "Judea Capta"—Judea is in captivity? Why else would Titus have built a triumphal arch at the place where the Jewish captives bearing the Menorah from the Temple were dragged into the Forum?[6]

Did Rome believe she was victorious over the God of Israel? After all, Rome was able to successfully break that bond between His people and His land. Perhaps they were thinking, just as God had predicted, "These are the people of the Lord, yet they have come out of His land." The nation of Israel remained scattered until this century, when God began to regather her.

The Years of Exile and Oppression

During almost two millennia of exile, Israel endured great persecution and frequently faced annihilation. Individual hatreds and local persecutions frequently ignited into mass murders of entire Jewish communities. When the Pope called European Christianity to mount a crusade to liberate the Holyland from the "infidels," the Crusaders began their "holy quest" with the murder of their local Jewish neighbors. When the Black Death ravaged Europe, another opportunity to exterminate the Jews appeared: Jews were accused of poisoning the wells and were murdered in towns throughout Europe.

Amazingly, Moslem-controlled Spain offered the Jews a brief respite from the storms of persecution. This was a

golden age for Jewish culture and scholarship. As the
Moslems were driven out of Spain, the Roman Church
felt the need to flex its power over the Spanish monarchy. Under the influence of the Spanish Inquisitors,
King Ferdinand and Queen Isabella signed an edict on
March 31, 1492, whereby the Jews were either forced to
convert or be expelled from Spain.

> No event since the destruction of Jerusalem
> fourteen centuries before had shaken the con-
> fidence of Jews everywhere more than the
> expulsion from Spain. Expulsion was not a
> new experience; Jews had been expelled from
> France, England, and many cities in Ger-
> many. But none of these events had a trau-
> matic effect in any way comparable to that of
> the sudden edict of banishment from Spain.
> Jews had never lived anywhere else as harmo-
> niously or creatively as in Spain. They had
> taken an active part in the life of Spanish
> society while also cultivating their own par-
> ticular legacy. They had been prominent in
> commerce, medicine, literature, and the arts.
> One out of every ten Spaniards had been Jew-
> ish or had descended from Jews. And now this
> flourishing community, the largest Jewish
> community in the world, had been eliminated
> with a single stroke of the pen. Jews every-
> where were reminded of their acute and ines-
> capable vulnerability.[7]

Anti-Semitism, which was originally fostered on tenuous theological grounds, took on an economic tone
during the Middle Ages. Europe was in a cash-poor
position due to a severe trade imbalance. Cash reserves
were depleted as Christian Europe indulged itself in
foreign wars and risky mercantile adventures to buy

Oriental luxury goods and spices. The Jewish community provided European nobility and merchants with the cash they needed. When the loans came due, the Christian debtors refused to pay not only the interest, but the principal as well. Laws were drafted, including the much-revered Magna Charta, to cancel Jewish claims on Christian estates. Great tension developed between the Christian and Jewish communities over these bad debts.

While the Protestant Reformation in Europe marks a return to the truth of the Word, it also marks the beginning of a new, virulent wave of anti-Semitism. Martin Luther was a leader of the German reform movement. While much of Europe remained staunchly Catholic, Germany in particular was profoundly influenced by Luther's teachings. On the one hand, he reintroduced the church to the doctrine of salvation through faith. On the other hand, he polluted German society with anti-Semitic invectives. In 1542 Luther published a pamphlet entitled "Against the Jews and their Lies":

> What then shall we Christians do with this damned, rejected race of Jews? Since they live among us and we know about their lying and blasphemy and cursing, we cannot tolerate them if we do not wish to share in their lies, curses, and blasphemy....
>
> First, their synagogues...should be set on fire, and whatever does not burn up should be covered or spread over with dirt so that no one may ever be able to see a cinder or stone of it....
>
> Secondly, their homes should likewise be broken down and destroyed. For they perpetrate the same things there that they do in their synagogues. For this reason they ought to be put under one roof or in a stable, like gypsies, in order that they may

realize that they are not masters in our land, as they boast, but miserable captives.

Thirdly, they should be deprived of their prayer books and Talmud in which such idolatry, lies, cursing, and blasphemy are taught.

Fourthly, their rabbis must be forbidden under threat of death to teach anymore.

Fifthly, passport and traveling privileges should be absolutely forbidden to the Jews. For they have no business in the rural districts since they are not nobles, nor officials, nor merchants, nor the like. Let them stay at home....

Sixthly, they ought to be stopped from usury. All their cash and valuables of silver and gold ought to be taken from them. For this reason, as said before, everything that they possess they stole and robbed from us through their usury, for they have no other means of support.

Seventhly, let the young and strong Jews and Jewesses be given the flail, the ax, the hoe, the spade, the distaff, and spindle, and let them earn their bread by the sweat of their noses as is enjoined upon Adam's children....

To sum up, dear princes and nobles who have Jews in your domains, if this advice of mine does not suit you, then find a better one so that you and we may all be free of this insufferable devilish burden—the Jews.[8]

Although separated by the centuries, the German National Socialists learned Luther's lesson well. On Kristallnacht (November 9-10, 1938), Jewish homes, businesses, and synagogues were destroyed and burned throughout German-controlled Europe. Subsequently all books, whether religious or secular, having Jewish authorship were burned by propaganda minister Joseph Goebbels; Jewish property was confiscated; and European Jewry was "collected under one roof" and placed in forced-labor camps.

Then, following Luther's recommendation to "find a better" way to make Europe "Judenrein"—free of Jews— the Nazis developed the "Final Solution." With the assistance of the indigenous population of Europe, Jewry was rounded up and sent to death factories designed for their efficient extermination. The Holocaust claimed the lives of 6 million Jewish souls—75 percent of European Jewry.

Of the 3.3 million Jews living in Poland, it is estimated that 3 million were murdered. Today, 50 years later, those national wounds are just now being addressed.

> In an unusual, emotional speech to the Israeli Parliament, President Lech Walesa of Poland apologized today for anti-Semitism in Polish history. "Here in Israel, the land of your culture and revival, I ask for your forgiveness," he told a chamber filled with Israel's leaders, some of them survivors of Auschwitz and other Nazi death camps built in Poland after the Germans overran the country, where three million Jews then lived.... "I am a Christian, and I cannot weigh with a human scale 20 centuries of evil for both of our people," he said.[9]

For two millennia Jewry had been used, abused, pillaged, hunted down, and murdered. The enemies of God had come ominously close to annihilating Israel, thus nullifying His ability to fulfill His promises. By the end of World War II, Jewry was dispirited and despoiled. Then God began to move in dramatic ways—God began to fulfill His promise to regather Israel a second time!

Dawn of the Messianic Age

At the same time that God revealed His plan to exile Israel, He also revealed His promise to regather her. The physical rebirth of the nation of Israel would be closely followed by her spiritual rebirth.

> I will take you from the nations, gather you from all the lands, and bring you into your own land. Then I will sprinkle clean water on you, and you will be clean; I will cleanse you from all your filthiness and from all your idols. Moreover, I will give you a new heart and put a new spirit within you; and I will remove the heart of stone from your flesh and give you a heart of flesh. And I will put My Spirit within you and cause you to walk in My statutes, and you will be careful to observe My ordinances (Ezekiel 36:24-27).

In this day, at this time, God has begun to fulfill His promises leading to the return of Messiah and the establishment of his kingdom. Let us now look at these two rebirths—the physical and the spiritual.

The Balfour Declaration

The starting gun for the kingdom-building process sounded with the Balfour Declaration in 1917. At that moment the reconstitution of the people and the land of Israel began. While God has been working to bless Israel with increased population and the bounty of the land, the nations have dealt her only betrayal and violence. Knowledge of these events gives us needed background for understanding developments in the Middle East today and in the future. The key to the ongoing violence in the Middle East is the organized effort to abort God's work of regathering His people and establishing them in His land.

Ever since their expulsion from Israel in 70 A.D., Jews around the world dreamed of returning to their land. In the late nineteenth century God aroused in the hearts of the Jewish people an unquenchable determination to return to Zion, or "Jerusalem." This determination took on form and organization; it became a movement called "Zionism." In 1897, Theodor Herzl organized the first World Zionist Congress. Leaders of this movement began consulting with heads of state regarding their desire. The British Government, sympathetic to Zionist objectives, originally offered the Jews a homeland in Uganda, of all places. This proposal was rejected, since there is no substitute for the ancient bond between the land of Israel and the sons of Israel. Diplomatic discussions and negotiations continued. This diplomatic path eventually led to Vatican City:

> The best interview of all was with the pope himself, on May 6. Benedict XV was an ardent Liberal who had been deeply perturbed by the persecutions of Jews in Eastern Europe. From the beginning of the conversation he made clear his sympathy with Zionism. "What a turn of destiny!" he said. "Nineteen hundred years ago Rome destroyed your homeland, and now, when you wish to rebuild it, you have chosen the path that leads to Rome." "I am deeply moved by such historical memories," Sakolow replied. "And may I be permitted to add that that Rome which destroyed Israel

was appropriately punished. Rome fell shortly afterward, whereas the people of Israel still live. They are so alive that now they even desire that their land be returned to them." "Yes," said the Pope. "It is Providential. God has willed it."[10]

After the end of World War I, in 1917, the British government wrote the following "letter of intent" called the Balfour Declaration:[11]

> Foreign Office,
> November 2nd, 1917.

Dear Lord Rothschild,

I have much pleasure in conveying to you, on behalf of His Majesty's Government, the following declaration of sympathy with Jewish Zionist aspirations which has been submitted to, and approved by, the Cabinet:

"His Majesty's Government view with favor the establishment in Palestine of a national home for the Jewish people, and will use their best endeavours to facilitate the achievement of this object, it being clearly understood that nothing shall be done which may prejudice the civil and religious rights of existing non-Jewish communities in Palestine, or the rights and political status enjoyed by Jews in any other country."

I should be grateful if you would bring this declaration to the knowledge of the Zionist Federation.

> Yours,
> Arthur James Balfour

Until the end of World War I, the Holyland had been under Ottoman Moslem control. The whole of the Middle East had been incorporated into one great empire without internal borders. With the defeat of the Axis and her Ottoman allies, the British saw the opportunity to establish the Jewish homeland in "Palestine." However, "Palestine" was a rather amorphous term and had to first be carved out of the vast Ottoman Empire. But regardless how vague, the Balfour Declaration raised hope in the Jewish community. Already there was a relatively large Jewish population in the Holyland. In 1917 Israel's demographics included approximately 45,000 Jews, 10,000 Moslems, and 15,000 Christians.

Israeli land is the perpetual inheritance of its original owners. In the law,[12] God commanded that land could never be sold, only leased. The price of the lease was to be adjusted relative to the number of years until the year of "Jubilee." A Jubilee occurred every 50 years and it marked a time when all land reverted to the original owners.

Here is an interesting thought for your consideration: In 1917 Israel had been living in exile for approximately 2500 years, since the time of the Babylonian Exile. The number 2500 is 50 times 50, or a Jubilee of Jubilees. Therefore the Balfour Declaration marked the beginning of the ultimate and final return of Eretz Yisrael, the land of Israel, to its original owners!

The British Mandate

The territory of the defeated Ottoman Empire had to be governed. Based upon the intent stated in the Balfour Declaration, the Supreme War Council gave Britain a mandate to caretake "Palestine" until an independent Jewish homeland could be created. That mandate included the territory which is today Israel and Jordan.

Then came the first act of treachery. In 1922 the League of Nations approved the British Mandate with

the provision that the portion of Palestine known as
Transjordania would be exempt from the commitments
of the Balfour Declaration. In keeping with this provision, Britain divided "Palestine." In 1928 the state of
Transjordan was created under the rule of the Hashe-
mite Dynasty. Through this division of the land, approximately three-quarters of the land held in trust for the
Jews was given to the Arabs.

Britain continued to administer the remaining quarter of the land, but with great difficulty. The Palestinian
Arabs hated the Jews. Consistent with all other enemies of God and Israel, they placed continuous pressure
on Britain to forbid or severely restrict Jewish immigration and the sale of land to Jews. This act became all the
more heinous in light of the growing persecution of Jews
in Hitler's Europe. Soon Arabs and Jews engaged in
open warfare.

The frustrated British called in their "management
consultants." After many studies, interviews, and much
analysis, a series of reports were released.

1930   *Sir Walter Shaw Report.* This study indicated
        that the source of the conflict was Arab hatred
        of Jews.

1930   *League of Nations Report.* This report con-
        demned the British for inadequate policing.
        This is interesting in light of the constant criti-
        cism which the Israeli government receives
        today when trying to control Arab violence.
        Britain may do well to remember its own
        inability to control Arab-Israeli violence the
        next time the Security Council is considering
        condemning the Israeli government for harsh
        policing tactics.

Later, in 1937, the British set up military courts to deal with terrorism. Members of the Arab High Committee were deported. Anyone caught carrying firearms or bombs was subject to a death sentence. Today Israel is condemned by the U.N. for deporting convicted murderers and merely arresting terrorists. Some nations are moving to hold Israel in contempt of the Geneva Convention.

1937 *Peel Commission Report.* This study determined that Jews and Arabs cannot live together in peace. It audaciously recommended further partitioning of the land. The remaining quarter of the original mandate would be divided into thirds: The Jews were to be given the coastal plains in the north, the British would retain a corridor from the port city of Jaffa to Jerusalem, including Bethlehem, and the Arabs would be given the rest.

Amazingly, the Jews accepted this twelfth portion of their mandated territory. The Arabs rejected the plan. They demanded that the British abandon the concept of a Jewish homeland and stop Jewish immigration. In exchange, they would "allow" the Palestinian Jews to remain as a "guaranteed minority."

1938 *Woodhead Commission Report.* This report reevaluated the concept of partitioning and determined that it was impractical. It recommended that a conference be held instead.

1939 *Palestine Conference.* This conference was convened and a British proposal was presented. It recommended that a joint Arab-Jewish Palestinian state be created within ten years. Within five years Jewish immigration would

have been stopped with a cap of 75,000 immigrants, and the sale of land to Jews would be
severely restricted. This plan was rejected by
both Arabs and Jews. By this time the Holocaust was in full swing, and the British in
Palestine turned away Jews fleeing death in
Europe.

The U.N. Usurpers

After 30 years of failure, the British gave up trying to
find a peaceful solution to creating a Jewish state in
Palestine. Britain had found the truth in the prophecy
that Jerusalem was "a heavy stone for all the peoples;
all who lift it will be severely injured."[13] In 1947 they
turned the "Palestine" issue over to the United Nations.

Following the lead of the Peel Commission Report,
the U.N. voted to partition the remaining quarter of
"Palestine" into an Arab and a Jewish state, and kept
Jerusalem for themselves, putting it under U.N. trust-
eeship. And just as with the Peel Commission report,
the Jews accepted the plan and the Arab League Council rejected it. So violent was the Arab rejection that the
Arab League Council announced that it would stop the
division of Palestine by force.

The Arab Boycott

Since 1948 Israel has been fighting for her life.
Reviewing these relatively recent events allows us to
understand why present-day negotiations of a Middle
East Peace Covenant have been so difficult and so
fraught with distrust. Assumptions which we often
make about who possessed what and when are often
wrong, since they are the product of a disinformation
campaign.

In advance of Israeli statehood, the Arab League began boycotting any corporation that had business ties with the Palestinian Jews. This boycott which began in 1946, is still in force today, and is gaining new relevance and causing renewed concern:

> Spurred by the fast-approaching economic unification of the European Community and encouraged by the close alliance between Kuwait, Saudi Arabia and the Western countries following the Gulf war, Israeli diplomatic officials are stepping up their efforts to dislodge the Arab boycott.... Officials are especially concerned that the boycott may gain strength through the wave of international mergers taking place in anticipation of the unification of the EC in 1992.... Both the European Community, as well as the European Free Trade Area (EFTA—the association of non-EC West European countries) are now negotiating a trade agreement with the Gulf Cooperation Council. Israeli diplomats are asking the Europeans to include an anti-discrimination clause in the agreements that would bar these states from imposing sanctions on European companies that trade with Israel.[14]

In 1948 the reborn nation of Israel declared her statehood and was immediately attacked by her Arab neighbors. The Western nations, many of whom recognized her statehood, betrayed her and let Israel twist in the wind:

> When the newly reborn State of Israel was fighting for its life, in 1948, it called the White House, begging for weapons with which to defend itself. President Truman didn't answer. The U.S. had declared an arms embargo

on the Middle East—meaning Israel, since
the Arabs were being armed to the teeth by
the British.[15]

Transjordan captured the territory of Judea and
Samaria—"the West Bank" and east Jerusalem. Looking forward to the day when they could finish Israel off,
the Palestine Congress adopted the Transjordanian king
as the "King of Palestine." To celebrate their unlawful
annexation, the nation changed its name from Transjordan ("across the Jordan") to Jordan, for now they
possessed both banks. During Jordan's occupation of this
land there was no world condemnation of its "occupation,"
there was no further talk of internationalizing Jerusalem,
Judea and Samaria were shown as part of Jordan on every
map, and there was no Jordanian Resolution 242. In fact,
it has become conventional wisdom that the West Bank
was Jordanian territory illegally captured by Israel during the Six-Day War. This is disinformation!

In this same war, Egypt illegally seized the Gaza
Strip. Israel was under siege for approximately 14 months,
but by the grace of her God and the courage of her
people, she survived. Then in 1956 Egypt nationalized
the Suez Canal and closed it to Israeli traffic.

In 1956, to halt the fedayeen raids from Egypt,
Israel joined England and France in their war
against Egypt to take control of the Suez Canal.
Though the allies were victorious, President
Eisenhower intervened so that England and
France relinquished their control of the Suez
Canal. Israel gave up the Sinai in exchange for
a "guarantee" that the U.S. would defend
Israel from any future attacks from Egypt.
The 1967 War proved that "guarantee" to be
absolutely worthless.[16]

Preempted War Plans

In the early to mid-1960's, the Arab nations began conspiring to divert the Jordan River before it entered Israel, and began to prepare a plan for the next war. As these plans and troop movements became an open secret, Israel was again betrayed by the West.

> In the spring of 1967, as the Arabs' noose tightened around Israel's neck, as Nasser closed the Straits of Tiran, as the Arab armies marched toward Israel's borders and the Arab leaders vowed to annihilate the Jewish State, the Israelis called the White House for assistance. President Johnson didn't answer. He had forgotten the promise that Eisenhower had made to the Israelis back in 1957, the promise that the U.S. would insure that the Straits of Tiran would stay open.[17]

The Arab nations sensed the approach of an opportunity to abort God's work and push the Jews into the sea. The Arabs prepared for war. Israel would be massively outnumbered and overwhelmed. The Jordanian "King of Palestine" looked forward to annexing the rest of Israel.

> King Hussein gave orders to his men that when Israel was defeated, every man, woman and child in Israel was to be killed. Nasser told the UN to vacate the buffer zone at the Sinai border with Israel and the UN complied instantly. The Arabs attacked, but with the help of G–d, the Israelis defeated the combined Arab forces within six days, reunited Jerusalem, and took Judea and Samaria and Gaza.[18]

In a brilliantly executed and desperate tactical move, Israel preemptively destroyed the Arab air forces on the ground. The war ended almost as quickly as it started, lasting only six days. Although vastly outgunned, Israel took back Judea, Samaria (the West Bank), East Jerusalem, and Gaza, and additionally captured the Sinai Peninsula from Egypt and the Golan Heights from Syria.

The Sinai Peninsula had a lower strategic importance, since it is a vast, uninhabited wasteland and offers a low military threat. This territory would eventually be returned to Egypt. On the other hand, the Golan Heights are just what their name indicates— high terrain that overlooks populated Israeli valleys. For 20 years this strategic high ground was used by Syria to bombard Israeli homes. Return of this territory, also known as ancient Bashan, is in doubt, for Jeremiah 50:19 says:

> I shall bring Israel back to his pasture, and he will graze on Carmel and Bashan, and his desire will be satisfied in the hill country of Ephraim and Gilead.

Israel is an incredibly small nation. Someone has said that it is the only nation in the Middle East that is so small that its name on a map has to be placed in the Mediterranean Sea. If you include the area of Judea and Samaria, Israel is approximately the size of San Bernardino County in California. In contrast, Arab lands total twice the size of the United States! When you remove Judea and Samaria from Israel, the area which contains 75 percent of its population and industrial sites becomes a mere nine miles wide. That this small scrap of land could be so hotly disputed is evidence that the problems in the Middle East are not about land, but are about stopping the work of God to restore and bless Israel.

The concept of creating a separate Palestinian State on "Israeli" territory, as proposed in the Peel Commission Report and others, was never acceptable to the

Arabs as long as they thought they could annihilate Israel. The urgency for creating a mythical Palestinian State only gained widespread acceptance after Israel regained strategic territory and her military conquest seemed less likely. The strategic importance of the Golan Heights and the West Bank is one of the major sticking points when negotiating Middle East peace. Both sides of the battle know that possession of these territories will make or break Israel.

Soon after Israel's resounding victory in the 1967 Six-Day War, the United Nations passed the now-infamous "Resolution 242." Conventional wisdom indicates that Resolution 242 states that Israel must return to its pre-1967 borders and that Israel is a renegade nation for not having abided by that resolution. More disinformation!

The following excerpt was written by Eugene V. Rostow, a fellow at the U.S. Institute of Peace, who helped write Security Council Resolution 242:

> Security Council Resolution 242, approved after the 1967 war, stipulates not only that Israel and its neighboring states should make peace with each other but should establish "a just and lasting peace in the Middle East." Until that condition is met, Israel is entitled to administer the territories it captured—the West Bank, East Jerusalem and Gaza Strip— and withdraw from some but not necessarily all of the land to "secure and recognized boundaries free of threats or acts of force." ... It prescribes that there should be no withdrawal until peace is made; then there can be a complete withdrawal, a partial one, or none, depending on what the parties decide.... Israel's new boundaries need not be the same as the armistice lines of 1949.[19]

This provision specifically addresses the problem of
peace with Jordan. Rostow continues:

> No state has title to the land between Israel
> and Jordan. Jordan's claim to have annexed
> the West Bank, never generally recognized,
> has been abandoned.... Israel has a stronger
> claim to the West Bank than any other nation
> or would-be nation because, under the League
> of Nations Mandate, Israel has the same legal
> right to settle the West Bank, Gaza Strip and
> East Jerusalem that it has to settle Haifa or
> West Jerusalem.

The Yom Kippur War

Arab machismo was severely damaged by the Six-
Day War. Another war was therefore inevitable. This
occurred on the holiest day of the biblical calendar in
1973, Yom Kippur.

> When Sadat succeeded Nasser in Egypt, Rus-
> sia convinced the Arab states to take another
> shot at Israel. That was the Yom Kippur War of
> 1973.... Israel's control of the Sinai, Judea
> and Samaria gave Israel an opportunity to
> mobilize and in a remarkably short time Israel
> managed to turn the tables.[20]

> As the Arabs prepared to invade in 1973, and
> Israeli intelligence detected the imminent at-
> tack, Prime Minister Golda Meir called the
> White House for help. Henry Kissinger warned
> her that if Israel launched a preemptive strike,
> the U.S. would give it no weapons. Golda suc-
> cumbed to the pressure, Israel suffered dev-
> astating losses, and the U.S. refused to give

Israel any weapons throughout the first 10 days of the fighting—Kissinger's way of making sure that the Israelis would not win too big a victory. Near the end of the 1973 war, when Israel had the Egyptian Third Army trapped in the Sinai Desert, and Israeli troops were on the road to Cairo, the Israelis made the mistake of calling the White House to consult—and Kissinger replied by pressuring them to halt their advances and release the trapped Egyptians.[21]

In 1978, U.S. President Carter brought together the leaders of Israel and Egypt to sign the Camp David Accords. Egypt became the only Arab nation to sign a peace treaty with Israel. In exchange for peace, the Sinai Peninsula was returned to Egypt. As a result of negotiating an independent deal with Israel, Egypt was ostracized from other Arab nations until 1989.

The Camp David booty has allowed the Egyptians to declare "victory" in the Yom Kippur War. On the road to the Cairo airport there is now a building called "The Panorama of the October 1973 War." This Arab monument may give insight into the change in the Egyptian mindset:

> The centerpiece . . . is a panel portraying the capture of the Bar-Lev line. At the heart of the panel are long rows of Israeli prisoners, heads bowed. In case the observer may have missed the point, the accompanying text states: "Israeli prisoners with heads bowed." It mentions also that as a result of the war, Egypt recovered all its lost territory "down to the last inch . . . including the city of Taba." One grasps from this how supremely important regaining Taba was to Egypt—it wasn't a kilometer of

sand with a luxury hotel, but "the last inch," whose recovery constitutes a central element of Egyptian national pride. For all the harrowing associations the panorama evokes, the exhibition also has a deeply satisfying message for an Israeli. It says that Egypt has purged itself of the humiliation of the Six Day War. It suggests that Egypt can deal with Israel rationally—that while it is an Arab state with Arab obligations, it no longer has a deep psychological need to strike back at Israel in order to erase its own scars.[22]

Defense of the North

In the late 1970's and early 1980's Israel was being regularly attacked across its northern border with Lebanon. Lebanon had become a PLO outpost, and a weapons cache for Syria and the Soviet Union. In 1982 Israel launched "Operation Peace for Galilee" and invaded Lebanon. The PLO was cornered and the weapons caches seized. The United States intervened on behalf of the Arabs and pressured Israel to allow the PLO to peacefully withdraw rather than be defeated.

What Nixon and Kissinger did for the Egyptians [in 1973], Reagan and Haig did for the PLO, pressuring Israel to lift its siege of Beirut in 1982 and refrain from wiping out Arafat and his hordes.[23]

By 1985 Israel withdrew from much of Lebanon, with the exception of a security zone in the south. Within two years the PLO began the "intifada," a movement to foment violent unrest within Israel's borders. The PLO received incredible sums of money from the Gulf States to finance their civil war. This bankrolling ended when the PLO backed Iraq against their Gulf patrons in the Gulf War.

The Second Return of Israel

In Ezekiel 37 the prophet relates how he was taken to a valley which contained the bones of the nation of Israel. God told Ezekiel to tell the bones that He would restore life and flesh to them. As Ezekiel spoke, he saw the bones assemble and ligaments grow to hold them together; muscles covered the bones and skin covered the flesh.

> I prophesied as He commanded me, and the breath came into them, and they came to life and stood on their feet, an exceedingly great army. Then He said to me, "Son of man, these bones are the whole house of Israel; behold, they say, 'Our bones are dried up, and our hope has perished. We are completely cut off.' Therefore prophesy, and say to them, 'Thus says the Lord God, Behold, I will open your graves and cause you to come up out of your graves, My people; and I will bring you into the land of Israel. Then you will know that I am the Lord, when I have opened your graves and caused you to come up out of your graves, My people. And I will put My Spirit within you, and you will come to life, and I will place you on your own land. Then you will know that I, the Lord, have spoken and done it,' declares the Lord" (Ezekiel 37:10-14).

The Zionist Movement

The Zionist movement began in the late nineteenth century. By the early twentieth century Israeli settlers began draining the malaria-infested swamps and planting forests to reclaim the land. It was a humble yet significant beginning. Then in the dark days of World War II, European Jewry faced extinction; six million Jews were "exterminated." Hitler and his minions attempted to abort this rebirth of Israel and seal Jewry in their graves. The British, who were administering the mandate, controlled and severely restricted Jewish immigration. In these desperate days Jews must have thought: "Our bones are dried up, and our hope has perished. We are completely cut off."

But then the bones began to rattle! The end of World War II was soon followed by Israeli statehood. Jews began to return in ever-increasing numbers. That which began as a trickle at the end of the nineteenth century has now become a flood. As Communism fell in 1989, the gates of all nations began to open. The government of Israel is today in peril because of their success— a tidal wave of Jewish immigrants which flow into it daily.

> "From the East and West, from Persia and Ethiopia, from Bukhara and Samarkand, and from Moscow and Kishinev, the Jews are coming to the only country that wants them and is waiting for them," said Counsul General Aryeh Levin as he raised the Israeli flag above Israel's Consulate in Moscow on Thursday.[24]

Since the fall of Israel to Rome, the majority of Jews have lived in the diaspora—dispersed among the Gentile nations.

> They will fall by the edge of the sword, and will be led captive into all the nations; and Jerusalem will be trampled under foot by the Gentiles until the times of the Gentiles be fulfilled (Luke 21:24).

The Days of the Gentiles

The days of the Gentiles have been fulfilled in our time. In 1967 Jerusalem was unified and became the capital of Israel. In keeping with the prophecy, God is leading the captives back to their land. With more and more Jews "making aliya"—"going up" or "ascending" to Israel—the majority of Jews may soon live in Israel:

> As a result of the Soviet aliya, it is likely that the majority of the world's Jews will be living in Israel in another 10 years, Prof. Sergio Della Pergola, a Hebrew University demographer, said last week. Only about 30 percent of world Jewry lives here now.[25]

In Ezekiel 36 God promises to multiply the men of Israel as part of his nation-building process. Truly this is what we are witnessing in our day:

> Thus says the Lord God, "On the day that I cleanse you from all your iniquities, I will cause the cities to be inhabited, and the waste places will be rebuilt."... Thus says the Lord God, "This also I will let the house of Israel ask Me to do for them: I will increase their men like a flock. Like the flock for sacrifices, like the flock at Jerusalem during her appointed feasts, so will the waste cities be filled with flocks of men. Then they will know that I am the Lord" (Ezekiel 36:33,37,38).

In that day, we are told by Jeremiah, the flight to Israel by the diaspora will be so dramatic that it will supersede the memory of the ancient exodus:

> "Therefore behold, the days are coming," declares the Lord, "when they will no longer say,

'As the Lord lives, who brought up the sons of
Israel from the land of Egypt,' but, 'As the
Lord lives, who brought up and led back the
descendants of the household of Israel from
the north land and from all the countries
where I had driven them.' Then they will live
on their own soil" (Jeremiah 23:7,8).

The Rescue Efforts

Since Israel became a state in 1948, there have been
numerous national efforts to rescue Jews from captivity,
all of them very heroic (see chart on next page). From
the mid-1980's through the early 1990's there have been
at least three major national emigrations—from Albania, Ethiopia, and the Soviet Union. In 1991, the entire
Jewish community of Albania immigrated to Israel. The
same year also witnessed the dramatic rescue of Ethiopian Jewry.

No one is certain about the origins of Ethiopian Jewry.
"Ethiopian Jewish tradition holds that the Jews descended from the leading families of Jerusalem who
accompanied Menelik, son of Solomon and the Queen
of Sheba, on his journey to Africa."[26] In any case,
their traditions are those of the first temple—Solomon's
Temple—which was destroyed 2500 years ago. These
Jews have been separated from the main body of Judaism for almost 3000 years, not knowing that there was a
new state of Israel or that there were any surviving
Jews apart from themselves. They have remained separate from Ethiopian society as well. The Ethiopians
disparagingly call them "Falashas" or "strangers."

In May of 1991, a heroic operation began which
sought to restore Ethiopian Jewry to the household of
Israel—"Operation Solomon." In an incredible exodus of
biblical proportions, 14,000 Jews were airlifted to Israel

Deliniation of Rescue Efforts

Year	Nation	Rescues	Known Remaining	Operation
1948-on	Romania	300,000		
1948-on	Syria	4,000	5,000	
1948-50	Yemen	45,000	few thousand	Operation Magic Carpet
1948-53	Egypt	10,000		Operation Goshen
1949-50	Iran	25,000	significant number	
1949-50	Afghanistan	4,000		
1949-50	Kurdistan	7,000		
1949-50	Iraq	110,000	several hundred	Operation Ezra and Nehemiah
1949-51	Libya	32,000		
1951	India	2,500		from the port city of Cochin
1950's	India	12,000		Bene Israel community
1953	Turkey	35,000	many	
1956	Egypt	12,000		
1959-65	Morocco	250,000		
1979	Iran	2,000	significant number	
1985-90	Ethiopia	20,000	many thousands	Operations Moses and Queen of Sheba
1989	USSR	250,000+	many thousands	ongoing
1991	Albania	300	0	
1991	Ethiopia	14,000	few thousand	Operation Solomon

in approximately 36 hours. At one point, 28 aircraft were in the air at the same time. "'We made history,' said Aryeh Oz, who piloted one El Al 747 cargo plane that carried more than twice as many passengers as it was designed to carry. 'It's the first time that any 747 or any air flying vehicle in the world ever carried 1,087 people. I don't think it will happen again.'"[27]

> The airlift proceeded through the night according to a complex schedule involving thousands of people in Israel and Ethiopia, the three dozen aircraft, and more than 400 buses at both ends. The bulk of it was carried out during the Jewish Sabbath, sundown Friday to sundown Saturday. But there were no complaints from the religious authorities; Jewish religious law allows and even encourages the violation of Sabbath observance if it is done to save lives. And in this case, the Sabbath actually made the operation easier since all the aircraft and buses used would have been idle.[28]

Those who witnessed the event knew this was a historic moment. The hand of God is almost tangible as He continues to regather His people.

> Pilots, flight attendants and others stood back with pocket cameras, smiling as they snapped reminders of "this historic moment," as all of them repeatedly called it. The sun began to rise just as the plane took off. Looking out the window, Yehoda Alamaho shook his head in wonder as he said, "I am so happy to be going to Israel after all this time." Chaim Gouri, an Israeli journalist aboard, was just as wondrous when he said, "They're ending a trip of 3,000 years."[29]

The children of Solomon had come home! What a privilege to behold the saving hand of God in action!

Soviet Union: Operation Exodus

The Soviet Union contained an extremely large community of Soviet Jews. Although they had been unable to openly practice their faith and observe Jewish law since the Bolshevik Revolution in 1917, they still retained their sense of community. The Soviets maintained strict control over all emigration, particularly that of Soviet Jewry. In that the Soviet Union was an Arab sponsor, this was consistent behavior. The cause—the freedom of Soviet Jewry—was adopted by some Western nations, particularly the United States. Their release was used as a bargaining chip in negotiations with the Soviets.

In the late 1980's, as the Soviet Union approached the edge of the abyss, it was forced to adopt perestroika and glasnost and to seek Western aid. To curry much-needed favor with the West, the Soviet Union began a measured release of Jews seeking to emigrate.

Jews all over the world sponsored "Operation Exodus," an operation to finance and facilitate the flight of Soviet Jewry. That operation has been a great success. Immigrants in numbers of biblical proportions have been returning to Israel, in spite of continued Soviet/Russian controls on emigration.

> This year [1991], 300,000 to 400,000 more Soviet Jews are expected. By 1993 or 1994, according to a study by four Israeli economists at Tel Aviv University, the influx of Soviet Jews will reach 1 million, and by the year 2000, 2 million. The study estimates that as a result of total immigration from all countries and natural increase the Jewish population of

Israel could climb to 7 million in this decade,
double the 3.5 million of 1990.[30]

Nearly as many Soviet Jews have arrived in
the last year as arrived in the 41 years since
independence in 1948. . . . Per capita, it's as if
the United States were to absorb France.[31]

On May 20, 1991, the Soviet Parliament enacted a
law allowing citizens to travel and emigrate freely
beginning in January 1993. That freedom marks a critical juncture in Russo-Israeli relations. As we discussed
earlier, the mass exodus of Soviet Jewry and the offense
taken by Russia's Arab clients could be a leading cause
of the Russo-Israeli War.

The American Enclave

With this mass emigration from Ethiopia, Albania,
and particularly the Soviet Union, the United States
now houses the largest community of Jews outside of
Israel. The Jewish community is very comfortable in
the United States, enjoying freedom of religion and en-
terprise. Ominously, "comfort" characterized Spanish
Jewry before the expulsions of 1492 and German Jewry
before the Holocaust. If this pattern continues, we might
expect that when the evil prince comes to power, the
United States may be the next site of extreme persecution of the Jewish people.

Israel, despite its problems with absorbing such a
massive influx of immigrants from the nations, is still
reaching out to her own around the world and calling
her children home:

The Soviet aliya is another sign of a new
age dawning in Jewish history, historic even
by Jewish history's outsize proportions. We

are witnessing the reversal of 2,000 years of Exile.... With the majority of Soviet Jews on their way here, God willing, there remains just one large pocket of Diaspora Jewry left: the North American continent.... Let my people come home! Never has Israel needed you more. Come with your talents, with your entrepreneurial spirit, with your capital, with your technology. Come with your financial wisdom, your sense of volunteerism, with your academic excellence, with your generous and democratic spirit. Come.[32]

The nation and people of Israel have been reborn, just as Ezekiel prophesied: "...and the breath came into them, and they came to life and stood on their feet, an exceedingly great army" (Ezekiel 37:10). The reborn Israel is a warrior nation. Some would say that she has the best army in the world. And just as the prophet wrote, as Israel has "stood on her feet," her power has terrified her enemies, and her continued growth has astonished even herself:

But virtually all Israelis, from politicians of the left and right to ordinary citizens, remain bewitched by the wave of immigration. They are awed by its dimension and confident that when all is said and done, it will bring strength, wealth and increased weight to Israel as a nation and as a military power in the Middle East.[33]

Building the Third Temple

Since 1967, when Israel gained control of Jerusalem and the Temple Mount, there has been a great debate:

whether or not to rebuild the temple. Although Jews pray three times daily, "May it be Thy will that the temple be speedily rebuilt in our days," some view the prospect of rebuilding the temple figuratively and others literally. In October 1989, Israel's Ministry of Religious Affairs sponsored "a first-ever Conference of Temple Research to discuss whether contemporary Jews are obligated to rebuild."[34] To some, it seems clear that if God has returned Israel to her land, then they are obligated by biblical commandment to begin building.

> "V'Assu Li Mikdash (Exodus 25:8)—And they shall make unto me a sanctuary" is a commandment that was given the Children of Israel when they were in the desert, on the way to the Promised Land. This Mitzvah [good deed] prevailed later as well, upon their entry into the Land of Canaan. In fact, it was one of the first three Mitzvot [good deeds] that the People of Israel were obligated to perform when they came to Eretz Yisrael.... When the modern Jewish renaissance culminated in the practical and victorious success with the establishment of the Zionist State of Israel, some individuals—who later developed into groups and movements—turned the dream of rebuilding the Beis HaMikdash [Temple] into real and serious hopes. Subsequently these hopes became plans, with quite a lot of practical detail, so much so that, if Moshiach were to come today, he would find all the plans and blueprints ready and the people prepared and willing to go ahead with the work immediately.[35]

Where Is the Holy of Holies?

At the forefront of the growing movement to rebuild the temple and restore temple worship is a group known as the Temple Mount Faithful. Under the leadership of Gershon Solomon, this group has consecrated stones and made several attempts to place them on the Temple Mount. Their efforts have always been aborted by Israeli police. But this has not dampened their spirit. When Gershon Solomon was recently asked what he would like to do given a free hand, he said:

> I would remove[36] the Moslem presence from the Temple Mount, announce to the world that the Temple Mount is the center of the Jewish People, and start building the Third Temple.[37]

Until 1983, conventional wisdom indicated that the Dome of the Rock—a large mosque in the center of the Temple Mount—was situated squarely on the site of the Jewish temple. In 1983, Asher S. Kaufman, a physics professor at Hebrew University, published an article in *Biblical Archaeology Review* entitled: "Where the Ancient Temple of Jerusalem Stood: Extant 'Foundation Stone' for the Ark of the Covenant is Identified."[38] Professor Kaufman, after extensive research, presented a convincing argument that the holy of holies was not located under the Dome of the Rock, but under a small cupola called the "Dome of the Tablets" and "Dome of the Spirits." This cupola, which resembles a small gazebo, lies on the large, vacant platform north of the mosque, directly opposite the Eastern Gate. It shelters a flat, exposed portion of Mount Moriah's bedrock. This exposed rock may have been the ancient resting place of the ark of the Covenant. In that the ark contained the tablets of the Ten Commandments, and was the place where the Spirit of God met man, the traditional names of this cupola support Kaufman's findings. While it may not be spiritually "preferable" for a mosque to share the Temple Mount with the Temple of God, Kaufman's research indicates that it would be possible to establish a place of worship on the site of the original holy of holies without regard to the Dome of the Rock.

We know from Daniel 9:27 and Matthew 24:15 that during the period of the seven-year Covenant there will be a holy place established in Israel which will be suitable for conducting biblically instructed sacrifice. Whether it is a stone temple or the refurbished tabernacle we are not told. However, in Revelation 11:2 there is a clue that the Dome of the Rock may be standing alongside this temple, for John is commanded to measure the temple:

> Leave out the court which is outside the temple, and do not measure it, for it has been given to the nations; and they will tread under foot the holy city for forty-two months.

Who Will Build the Temple?

In some rabbinical traditions, the next temple will not be built with human hands, but God will "build it with fire":

> Everyone of us is praying, crying, that G–d will bless us to again have the Beis Hamikdosh [Temple]—but it is not in our hands to build it. We have to wait until we are blessed by G–d as we are promised—"Ato Hashem be-eish hitzato uve-eish ato atid livnoto." "G–d, who burned the Beis Hamikdosh, will build the third Beis Hamikdosh with fire." Only G–d can build the third Beis Hamikdosh.[39]

This rabbinical tradition is somewhat disturbing in light of the text of Revelation 13:13,14. It is possible that the evil prince and his cabinet chief will exploit this tradition in order to validate their false messianic credentials. What would people think if these two men were able to call down fire from heaven and "create" a temple?

> He [the false prophet, the evil prince's cabinet chief] performs great signs, so that he even makes fire come down out of heaven to the earth in the presence of men. And he deceives those who dwell on the earth because of the signs which it was given him to perform in the presence of the beast, telling those who dwell on the earth to make an image to the beast who had the wound of the sword and has come to life (Revelation 13:13,14).

Some Christians, citing the efficacy of Messiah's sacrificial death, view with contempt Jewish desires and plans to rebuild the temple of God and begin sacrifice. They say that temples and sacrifices are passe. However, God Himself has provided the plans for another temple which has not yet been built. Some refer to this temple, described in Ezekiel chapters 40-45, as the millennial temple, for it will be built and functioning during the thousand-year messianic kingdom. This temple will not only be a site of worship, but a site of blood sacrifice as well. Ezekiel 46 describes in great detail the sacrifices and burnt offerings that God will require of the priesthood and the prince of Israel during that period. These sacrifices are different from those prescribed in the law. Some have suggested that these sacrifices are a remembrance of what Messiah has done, much like the bread and wine that Christians symbolically use in their remembrance services.

The Next Events

As we originally stated, all major milestone events lie on the Israeli pathway. The next steps on this pathway hold—

- ♦ a disadvantageous Middle East Peace Covenant;
- ♦ persecution when the kingdom of the evil prince is established and the prince sits in the temple of Israel's God;
- ♦ massive assaults during both the Russo-Israeli War and Armageddon;
- ♦ the establishment of the messianic and eternal kingdoms.

Even though these are major milestone events, it is unlikely that we would observe significant trends leading to them on the Israeli pathway, for in each of these events Israel is either a victim or passive onlooker. Observable trends which lead to these milestone actions are found on other pathways; Israel only "reacts." Despite this absence of significant trends, some divine preparations are indeed underway.

The Coming Menu

When God delivered Israel from Egyptian slavery, the Israelites were forced to wander in the wilderness for 40 years due to their sin. But God did not force them to forage for their own food. As any good father, He provided His children with a daily meal of manna and quail—a bit boring, but completely life-sustaining. When the evil prince comes to power, Israel will be pursued and forced to live in the mountains of Judea for

42 months. Just as God stocked the wilderness pantry with quail to sustain the millions who fled Egypt, God seems to be preparing His menu for Israel's flight to the mountains:

> The most amazing thing about the chukar partridges, *Alectoris chukar*, is that there are so many of them. Wherever you go in the hilly regions of Israel you see them.... The reason their numbers are surprising is that the late autumn to early spring hunting season is largely concentrated on this species. In addition, at least 50 percent of their nests—a shallow bowl scooped out on the ground—are destroyed by predators, for the chukar is a most important part of the food chain that nurtures most small predators. But despite this there are plenty of them about.... The female lays anywhere from six to 20 small speckled eggs and broods on them for 26 days. ... If a nest is destroyed by a fox or other predator, and if it isn't very late in the season, the pair will most often start a new brood, although these replacement broods are usually smaller, about six to 12 eggs. Although the male usually leaves the female when she begins to brood, cases have been known in which a single female laid two clutches of eggs and the male brooded on one of them. No one knows exactly what circumstances elicit this behavior.[40]

Birds of a different feather will not appear on the menu, but will be sitting at God's feasting table. In Ezekiel 39:17-20 the invitation is issued to come and feast on the fallen invaders of the Russo-Israeli War:

> As for you, son of man, thus says the Lord God, "Speak to every kind of bird and to every beast

of the field, 'Assemble and come, gather from
every side to My sacrifice which I am going to
sacrifice for you, as a great sacrifice on the
mountains of Israel, that you may eat flesh
and drink blood'" (Ezekiel 39:17).

In preparation for this great feast, God has been mul-
tiplying his invited guests. Every spring and fall
15 million raptors—birds of prey—commute through
Israel on their way to or from their homelands.

> European buzzards migrating southeast meet
> up with flocks flying southwest from Afghani-
> stan. From Turkey and Russia rise eagles,
> falcons, jackdaws, and storks to join them—
> nearly 300 species in all. An estimated 15
> million birds migrate annually from Europe
> and Asia south to Africa along a narrow land
> corridor—Eretz Yisroel. All this takes place
> in late September and early October.... The
> prophet Ezekiel in two chapters (38 and 39)
> foretells the attack by Gog, King of Magog,
> and his allies upon an Eretz Yisroel rebuilt
> and resettled.... The tenth sentence of the
> haftora (39:4) is addressed to Gog: "You will
> fall on the mountains of Yisroel, you and all
> your troops and the many nations that are
> with you; to the birds of prey on the wing and
> the animals of the wild have I given you to be
> eaten."... How convenient of G–d to have
> some 15 million raptors overfly Eretz Yisroel
> every Sukkos [Feast of Tabernacles] ready for
> this tremendous feast predicted more than
> 2,300 years ago![41]

Preparing the Way

In addition to preparing for days of persecution and
war, God is also preparing the way for the messianic

kingdom. It is interesting that as Messiah prepares to establish his kingdom in Jerusalem, the three thousandth anniversary of David's conquest of Jerusalem is almost upon us. This will surely be viewed as a sign of the messianic era. Perhaps the evil prince will seek to exploit this anniversary for his own "messianic" purposes.

> Teddy Kollek's foreign advisers gathered around him last month, to help begin planning celebrations in 1996 to mark the 3,000th anniversary of David's conquest of Jerusalem.... Although David's conquest of Jerusalem and his establishment there of his capital is generally attributed to 1,000 BCE, Kollek is relying on recent scholarly advice that the event more likely took place in 1,004 BCE. This conveniently sets the anniversary in 1996, separating Jerusalem's celebration, which aspires to worldwide reverberations, from the end-of-millennium celebrations that will be occupying the world's attention four years later.[42]

Perhaps in preparation for the coming of the King, archeologists have made another exciting discovery in recent years. Israel now possesses an ancient jug of balsam oil that could be used to anoint their messianic King. God had hidden this oil away for 2000 years. In early 1989 it was released to the press that—

> Israeli archeologists, searching caves near the Dead Sea, have discovered what they believe is a 2,000-year-old jug of once-fragrant oil of the kind used to anoint the ancient Israelite kings. Even though the oil is thought to have been placed in its earthen container at the time of Jesus, it was still fluid and had

maintained its original chemical composition, though it had lost its fragrance.[43]

The Spirit at Work

In addition to promising to regather Israel and establish them in their own land, God also promised to put His Spirit in them. As a result of this new Spirit they would be able to recognize the moving of the hand of God in the lives of the people.

> "I will put My Spirit within you, and you will come to life, and I will place you on your own land. Then you will know that I, the Lord, have spoken and done it," declares the Lord (Ezekiel 37:14).

Israeli statehood not only fulfilled the Zionist dream of a Jewish homeland, but it also began the fulfillment of this promise. Jews have begun to realize that the messianic age is about to dawn. "We have no prophets among us today, but students of the Bible can easily see that the day of redemption is coming closer."[44] As Rabbi Meir Kahane wrote before his assassination:

> One who lives and looks about and considers and contemplates the extraordinarily awesome events of the past 50 years and does not understand that here is the Divine hand of the Almighty moving His world into the final chapter, is either blind beyond hope of vision or a stiff-necked soul who deliberately refuses to see and acknowledge.[45]

While a number of years ago the moving of the hand of God may only have been recognized by those considered "religious," today that recognition is at a grass-roots level. All Israel has been awestruck by the divine intervention evidenced in two major events—the dramatic ingathering of the exiles and the Persian Gulf War.

> According to Menachem Brod, spokesman for Habad in Israel, the expectation that the arrival of the Messiah is imminent arises from a series of signs which have appeared over the past few decades.... Even the establishment of the State of Israel, Brod said, could be viewed as part of the preparation for salvation. True, he said, Habad did not share the view of religious Zionists who view the establishment of the state as "the first flowering of our redemption," but certainly the fact that all Jews could come to the Land of Israel was significant.[46]

Prophecy Fulfilled

The Prime Minister of Israel has publicly declared that the massive immigrations which his nation is experiencing are a fulfillment of biblical prophecy:

> The current waves of Jewish immigration to Israel are a fulfillment of Biblical prophecy, Prime Minister Yitzchak Shamir declared in his address to the nation on Israel's Independence Day. The immigration from Russia, Ethiopia, and Albania is the fulfillment of the words of Isaiah: "I will bring your offspring from the East and gather you from the West; to the North, I will say, 'Give them up, and the south. Do not hold them.'"[47]

The chemical threat to Israel during the Gulf War which caused them to live in sealed rooms was also viewed as a direct fulfillment of prophecy:

The Prophet Isaiah in chapter 26, verse 20, foretold the present-day danger to the people of Israel. According to the Radak, in the time of the wars of Gog U'Magog...there will be danger. Therefore, the Prophet Isaiah advises: "Go, my people, enter your room, close and seal the door and hide therein for a moment until the danger passes." (This is happening today.) The Prophet continues: "Then the L–rd will come forth and punish the sinners (the murderers) for their iniquity and the earth shall no more cover those who were slain (the Jews)." The murderers will be punished.[48]

In the tense moments before the Gulf War, "over 25,000 Jews flocked to the Western Wall under heavy police protection Monday afternoon to pray for G–d's help in enduring the safety of the Jewish people if war breaks out.... Calling on people to pray to G–d to 'save us from those who rise up against us,' the poster quoted the verse from Psalms: 'Some depend on horses and some on chariots, but we invoke the Name of G–d our L–rd. They stumble and fall, but we are risen and stand firmly.'"[49] Israel sought the protection of her God and received it!

The Coming Age

The divine and miraculous protection which Israel enjoyed during the Gulf War has been viewed as a major sign of the coming messianic age. Belief in the imminent advent of Messiah has excited Jewish desires and cries for redemption now!

Most Jews believe in the coming of Moshiach [Messiah]. But often it has become a dry, abstract belief, just mumbling over the "Ani

Maamin" by rote. By realizing how we have
witnessed supernatural miracles, we now have
a Heaven-sent opportunity to bring our belief
in the Moshiach to life. Even more vividly can
our belief in Moshiach be brought to life by
studying Torah subjects about Moshiach and
the Messianic age.... Now it depends only on
us. We have all seen the miracles. All we need
do now is believe with all our hearts in the
coming of Moshiach and to implore the Almighty—and really mean it—to bring the
geula [redemption] immediately. It is essential that those with access to the media, like
writers and newspaper editors, should now
utilize their full talents to bring the message
of these miracles to the widest possible public....
All Jews, especially writers and editors, have
have the sacred duty to help create a storm of
public opinion that will demand of the Almighty: After all Your amazing miracles,
please, please, keep Your promise by bringing
us the Moshiach NOW![50]

The Steps Ahead

The Israeli pathway is a busy one. We will soon encounter each of the milestones and intersect every other
pathway. The steps until the midpoint of the Covenant
are already clear:

- Israel has been reborn in Eretz Yisrael,

- her children—cast to the four winds—are
  returning home, most dramatically, Soviet
  Jewry (those held by "Gog") and Ethiopian
  Jewry (those held by "Cush"),

- she is actively preparing for the reinstitution of Temple service,

- she is being fitted for an economic noose by the forming European Empire, and

- she is being increasingly pressured to enter into a Middle East Peace Covenant that will once again attempt to break the divine bond between the Land and the People of God.

Seeing Further

At this late hour on God's timepiece, it should come as no surprise that even more distant steps on the Israeli pathway are coming into view. The steps which fall between the midpoint of the Covenant and the establishment of the messianic kingdom are appearing out of the mists of time. These include stepped-up activity by the usurpers and the abortionists:

- The rise of anti-Semitism on a world scale.

- Jerusalem becoming—

    —the seat of the evil prince's kingdom and the site of his deification.

    —"a cup that causes reeling to all the people around."[51] The Arab nations are intoxicated with the thought of repossessing the City of God and are prepared for war, allied first with Gog and then with the evil prince.

    —"a heavy stone for all peoples; all who lift it will be severely injured."[52] Jerusalem is a diplomatic dilemma that all foreign ministers feel compelled to address.

—an international "outlaw." Jerusalem is
consistently condemned by the world community; soon the "Desert Storm Encirclement Plan" will be dusted off and called
"Operation Armageddon."

- The demand for fulfillment of the promise of
the Messiah and the dream of the messianic
kingdom becoming a tangible reality.

Soon the usurpers and abortionists will be the stuff of
history—the unholy, gruesome, prekingdom history of
mankind! Israel's prophets, priests, and kings longingly
looked forward to the arrival of Messiah and the establishment of His kingdom. Think of them! Abraham,
Isaac, Jacob, Moses, Aaron, David, Solomon, Isaiah,
Ezekiel, Zechariah, and all the other faithful servants
of God prayed that they might see His coming. And by
the evidence before us, it would appear that you and I
will be the ones privileged to witness His return. We are
truly a blessed generation!

The Mounting Drama

We can see the hand of God moving in the most visible
ways:

- He has reestablished His people in their
land.
- He is regathering His people a second time
from the four corners of the earth in the
most dramatic ways.
- He has ensured Israel's victory in battle.
- He has renewed in the hearts of His people
the hope of the messianic promise.

There is electricity in the air! The signs of Messiah's
arrival are so numerous that the promise is becoming

tangible. The coming of Messiah is no longer a dry doctrine or a repetitious prayer. The voices of Jews and Christians are joined in prayerful petition that God will complete His messianic promises now. As we soberly consider the sins which will be committed against God's people and His city between now and the beginning of the messianic kingdom, let us share in the song of David in Psalm 122:6: "Pray for the peace of Jerusalem: may they prosper who love you."

Let us comfort ourselves in knowing that our God reigns—now and throughout eternity!

A FINAL CHALLENGE

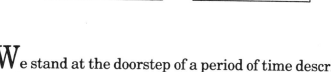

We stand at the doorstep of a period of time described in the Bible as "last days." The crowning event of those days is the coming of Messiah. But before the coming of Messiah and the establishment of his thousand-year kingdom, a usurper will arise. This usurper messiah will be the evil prince, and his usurper kingdom will be a European-based world empire. After oppressing God's people, he will meet his doom when he attempts to frustrate the return of Israel's true Messiah.

We have been examining significant geopolitical trends in history and in our day. Those trends are rapidly leading us to those last days. We have seen how:

- ◆ The pathway of government is leading away from the nation-state and in the direction of world government—the kingdom of the evil prince.

- ◆ The pathway of power is turning toward the centralization of world power in the hands of a single man—a monarch—the evil prince or "Antichrist."

- ◆ The pathway of Europe is ever broadening and is in the process of mounting an economic takeover of the planet.

- The Russian pathway is in a dangerous downward spiral which will culminate in the Russo-Israeli War.

- The Arab/Moslem pathway is being detoured by God to judgment. Some Moslem nations will follow the Russian lead and meet their judgment as they fall in battle on the hills of Judea. Other Moslem nations will have their judgment individually meted out by God, all resulting from their treatment of Israel, God's people.

- The Israeli pathway is about to become well-traveled, or rather "well-trampled." The nations of the world, led by the evil prince, will soon cross this path as the Middle East Peace Covenant is imposed. That landmark event will be quickly followed by the occupation of Israel by the evil prince, the calling of all nations to encircle Israel at the battle of Armageddon, and the triumphal coming of her Messiah and His kingdom.

Knowing these things, what should be our response? As privileged members of the Christian community who have been given insight into the days that lie before us, what should be our pathway? Through inattention we often meander through life without regard to the path on which we are walking. We are so enthralled and occasionally overcome by the events going on around us that we are guided by them, much like a child following moths through a forest. At the end of the day we are surprised where it has led us.

We must not allow the path of our life to become an accident of undirected, daily wanderings. When we aimlessly wander, we will undoubtedly walk the way of the desires of the flesh, since this comes so naturally to our fallen natures. It is only through hard work that we can walk in the way of the Spirit and set our feet on the path that leads to the kingdom of God.

Liberating Power

Without the power of the indwelling Spirit of God, all mankind is condemned to walk in the flesh. However, the salvation provided to us through Messiah has liberated us from the flesh. God has provided us with the indwelling Spirit of God by which He has empowered us to live holy lives. By calling us to holiness, we are also called to forsake the way of the flesh. You cannot walk in the flesh and the Spirit concurrently, for they lead in opposite directions.

The apostle Paul counseled the believers at Galatia to rid their lives of the deeds of the flesh:

> Walk by the Spirit, and you will not carry out the desire of the flesh. For the flesh sets its desire against the Spirit, and the Spirit against the flesh; for these are in opposition to one another, so that you may not do the things that you please. But if you are led by the Spirit, you are not under the Law. Now the deeds of the flesh are evident, which are: immorality, impurity, sensuality, idolatry, sorcery, enmities, strife, jealousy, outbursts of anger, disputes, dissensions, factions, envying, drunkenness, carousing, and things like these, of which I forewarn you just as I have forewarned you that those who practice such things shall not inherit the kingdom of God (Galatians 5:16-21).

These deeds are so prevalent in our society that they have unfortunately become its fabric. Today the major church denominations are being tempted by factions within them to forsake the standard of holiness set before us by our God, and instead accept the standards of the society around us. The choice is clear: We can live by the standards of our God and call society higher, or we can forsake our God and wallow in the sinful mire with the rest of mankind. Pray that we as individuals and that our organized churches choose wisely, for the consequences are great.

If we habitually practice the works of the flesh, we must thoughtfully question whether we have truly had a salvation experience. For if our turning to the Lord empowers us through the indwelling Spirit to overcome the flesh, but our lives in no way evidence that power, then we have no cause to rest in the comfort of that questionable salvation. To repeat the apostle Paul's warning: "I have forewarned you that those who practice such things shall not inherit the kingdom of God."

Let us each examine our lives. First, we must be certain of our salvation, for without that salvation we are lost. Once confident of that commitment, let us open our lives to the Spirit of God and allow Him to do some housekeeping within us. We must make the commitment to *facilitate* rather than *frustrate* His work.

Let us not hesitate to take action when He shows us how to reprioritize our lives, how to prune away our "deeds of the flesh," and how to refocus our lives on the achievement of God's purposes. The hour is late, and our Lord is coming. There is no time for dawdling; it is time to clean house.

Walking in the Spirit

Walking in the Spirit, because it is contrary to our nature, is hard work. It requires commitment and our constant attention. But our reward is citizenship in the kingdom of God. What are some of the things that we might do to prepare for walking in the Spirit?

First, we must study the Word of God. Our study should not have as its object the mere accumulation of facts, but rather *knowledge of the Author*. This should not be a superficial knowledge of His works, but a deep insight into His personality and His nature. Such knowledge of Him will beget a deeper love for Him. Second, we must spend more time in prayer. As believers in Messiah, we stand as kings and priests before God. If we are priests, then it is our responsibility to engage in intercession on behalf of the society in which we live. Our society needs the salvation of God. The only reason that God has forestalled the coming of His kingdom is to allow mankind a few more moments to accept His grace. Pray that people might open their hearts to God and His Messiah. Pray that the redeeming power of our God will change the lives of people in our day.

Anyone who reads a newspaper must mourn for the society in which we live. Is there any question that people need their lives transformed by the living and loving God? Is there any question that we need God's help to survive and overcome these perilous times? The apostle Paul described the sinful nature of these times:

> Realize this, that in the last days difficult times will come. For men will be lovers of self, lovers of money, boastful, arrogant, revilers, disobedient to parents, ungrateful, unholy, unloving, irreconcilable, malicious gossips, without self control, brutal, haters of good, treacherous, reckless, conceited, lovers of pleasure rather than lovers of God; hold to a form of godliness, although they have denied its power; and avoid such men as these (2 Timothy 3:1-5).

Laboring in prayer is hard work, but living in these days without the direction and assistance of God is harder!

Third, let us exercise discernment in everything we do, from settling doctrinal differences to family squabbles. As we said, through Messiah we stand as kings and priests before our God. As kings or rulers during the messianic kingdom, we will be called upon to make decisions and judge between men. That skill which we will require in the kingdom we can surely use in our life here on earth as well.

To be sure, none of these things is easy! However, when we begin the hard work of walking in the Spirit, God actively supports us. He is a loving Father and knows that the going is tough for His children. He has already provided us with His indwelling Spirit to empower us. When we acknowledge His sovereignty in the details of our lives, He promises to provide us with direction as well.

> Trust in the Lord with all your heart, and do not lean on your own understanding. In all your ways acknowledge Him, and He will make your paths straight (Proverbs 3:5,6).

As we do these spiritual calisthenics, we will begin to see the fruit of our labor. For just as walking in the flesh bears the fruit of immorality, sensuality, and hostility, so walking in the Spirit bears an outward, recognizable fruit. The bearing of that fruit is confirmation that we belong to Jesus.

> The fruit of the Spirit is love, joy, peace, patience, kindness, goodness, faithfulness, gentleness, self-control; against such things there is no law. Now those who belong to Christ Jesus have crucified the flesh with its passions and desires (Galatians 5:22-24).

A righteous life which brings glory to our Lord is not just characterized by the absence of sin, but also by the presence of the works of God. Allow God to touch your life; allow Him to touch others through you.

Rekindled Desire

When we are walking in the Spirit, we will discover a rekindled desire for Messiah and His kingdom. It is right and good to desire the coming of the Kingdom of God and the working out of God's will upon the earth. When His disciples asked Jesus how to pray, He instructed them to express this very desire:

> Our Father who art in heaven, hallowed be Thy name. Thy kingdom come. Thy will be done on earth as it is in heaven. Give us this day our daily bread. And forgive us our debts, as we also have forgiven our debtors. And do not lead us into temptation, but deliver us from evil. For Thine is the kingdom, and the power, and the glory, forever. Amen (Matthew 6:9-13).

Jesus was instructing us to synchronize our desire for the kingdom with God's intention to establish it. He was also instructing us to desire the order and justice that will prevail when Messiah reigns and God's will is worked out upon the earth. Instead of being moved to anger or despair when we read the newspapers, let us use those murders, rapes, and abuse of children to sharpen our desire for the reign of Messiah. The news should drive us to prayer.

In addition to desiring the kingdom, we must also rekindle our desire for Messiah Himself. What bride is not exhilarated as her wedding day approaches? What lover is not breathless at the thought of her beloved?

Soon, at the rapture, we will meet our Beloved. Together we will journey to the New Jerusalem for the royal wedding—the wedding of King Jesus and His bride-queen. For seven years we will celebrate our marriage feast with the heavenly host. While the earth is beset by the reign of the evil prince, we will experience unspeakable joy in the presence of our Beloved.

Let us restore passion to our relationship. Let us desire our Lord's presence as that of an absent loved one. Let us study His life and teachings that we might know Him better. Let us rejoice in biblical doctrine as it is transformed into a living reality—a promise of God. Let us rediscover the excitement and the joy of anticipating the soon arrival of our beloved Lord and coming King.

Our anticipation and desire can only be exceeded by that of our Lord Himself. Before His suffering and death, His thoughts were of us. He interceded for us, praying:

> Father, I desire that they also, whom Thou hast given Me, be with Me where I am, in order that they may behold My glory, which Thou hast given Me; for Thou didst love Me before the foundation of the world. O righteous Father, although the world has not known Thee, yet I have known Thee; and these have known that Thou didst send me; and I have made Thy name known to them, and will make it known; that the love wherewith Thou didst love Me may be in them, and I in them (John 17:24-26).

Share the Light

As we desire the presence of our Lord, we will naturally watch and wait for Him. As we study the word of the prophets, we will know and recognize the signs of His coming. Our studies will provide us with insight that will not be shared by the society around us.

> Go your way, Daniel, for these words are con-
> cealed and sealed up until the end time. Many
> will be purged, purified and refined; but the
> wicked will act wickedly, and none of the
> wicked will understand, but those who have
> insight will understand (Daniel 12:9,10).

And how is that insight obtained? Through God's
Word, for His Word is a lamp to our feet and a light to our
path (Psalm 119:105). We must share that insight with
our neighbors and offer them redemption from judgment and the fear of the unknown.

We have a message of hope for the world. As the world
seems to be spinning off its physical and moral axis,
we have the knowledge and comfort that our God is sovereign. When the world offers fear, we can offer hope
and comfort. When the world lies condemned, we can
offer salvation through Messiah. When the world offers
despair, we can offer direction. When the world offers a
kingdom of despair, we can offer a kingdom of peace and
justice—Messiah's coming kingdom.

As the world sees the pathways to Armageddon becoming increasingly clear, the days will be filled with
fear and darkness. It is our responsibility to share our
hope with the world, for by the grace of God we can see
beyond Armageddon: We can see the everlasting kingdom of our God!

Notes

Chapter 2—Prophetic Milestones

1. The English word "antichrist" is itself deceiving, for the prefix "anti-" gives us the sense of "against." Actually, the literal translation means "*instead* of Christ." I prefer to think of him as the "Almostchrist." Apart from the true Messiah Himself, this man will appear to be the best hope the world has to offer. Rather than being totally opposite or against Messiah, he will be a great counterfeit.
2. Daniel 9:24,27.
3. J. Dwight Pentecost, *Things to Come* (Zondervan, 1958), p. 244.
4. Ibid., p. 245.
5. John 3:29; Revelation 19:7-9.
6. Zola Levitt, *A Christian Love Story* (Zola Levitt Ministries, 1978), pp. 1-6.
7. Matthew 24:37-39; Luke 17:26,27.
8. Luke 17:28-33.
9. 1 Corinthians 15:50-58.
10. 1 Corinthians 9:24-27; 2 Timothy 4:7,8; 2 Corinthians 4:10; 1 Corinthians 3:12-15.
11. 1 Corinthians 3:12-15.
12. 1 Thessalonians 5:2.
13. *Atlas of the Bible Lands* (Hammond Inc., 1959), p. B-4.
14. Hal Lindsey, *The Late Great Planet Earth*, (Zondervan, 1970), p. 65.
15. Jeremiah 30:7; cf. KJV.
16. Daniel 9:26.
17. Daniel 9:26.
18. Daniel 7:3; Revelation 13:1.
19. Daniel 7:23.
20. Daniel 8:25.
21. Revelation 13:3,4,16,17.
22. Revelation 17:12,13.
23. Revelation 17:12.
24. 2 Thessalonians 2:4.
25. Revelation 11:3-13; Zechariah 4.
26. Zechariah 14:4,5,9.
27. Revelation 19:20; Daniel 11:45.
28. Matthew 25:31-36.
29. Revelation 20:4.
30. Isaiah 2:2-4.
31. Revelation 21:9,10.
32. Revelation 20:4.
33. 2 Timothy 2:11-13; Revelation 5:10; 20:4-6.
34. Revelation 21:9-11.
35. Jeremiah 30:9; Ezekiel 34:23,24; 37:24,25; Hosea 3:5.
36. Revelation 5:9,10.
37. Isaiah 65:17-25.
38. Revelation 19:15.
39. Revelation 20:7.
40. Revelation 20:8.
41. Revelation 20:9,10.
42. Revelation 21 and 22.

Chapter 3—Intriguing Detours

1. "Central Asia Rediscovers Its Identity," in the *New York Times*, June 24, 1990.
2. "Goodbye to the Nation-State," in *The Economist*, June 23, 1990.
3. Ibid.
4. Ibid.
5. Ibid.
6. Ibid.
7. "Bureaucratic United Nations Finds Budget Reform Elusive," *Insight*, Jan. 21, 1991.
8. "Goodbye to the Nation-State," *The Economist*, June 23, 1990.
9. "Rising Party in Italy's North Wants to Get Rome and the South Off its Back," in the *New York Times*, June 24, 1990.
10. "Goodbye to the Nation-State," in *The Economist*, June 23, 1990.
11. "Rising Party in Italy's North Wants to Get Rome and the South Off its Back," in the *New York Times*, June 24, 1990.
12. "Goodbye to the Nation-State," in *The Economist*, June 23, 1990.
13. Robert. A. Dahl, *Democracy and Its Critics* (Yale University Press, 1989) p. 319.
14. "Uncalm Currencies." in *The Economist*, Feb. 16, 1991.
15. Dahl, *Democracy*, p. 313.
16. "Reality Sets In: No one ever said freedom would be easy," in the *World Press Review*, Feb. 1991.
17. "Special Report: Seeking a New World, 2. Can Universal Democracy Work?" in the *Los Angeles Times*, Dec. 11, 1990.
18. Ibid.
19. Dahl, *Democracy*, chapter 4.
20. Ibid., p. 57.
21. Ibid., p. 52.
22. Ibid., p. 76.
23. Ibid., p. 78.
24. Ibid., p. 320.
25. "Can Kings Replace the Commissars?" in *Royalty*, Jan. 1991.
26. Ibid.
27. Ibid.
28. Ibid.
29. Ibid.
30. Ibid.
31. Ibid.
32. "Raising the Royal Horizons," in *Royalty*, Jan. 1991.
33. "I'm someone who listens to my heart, not my head: Prince Charles on French TV," in *Royalty*, Feb. 1991.

Chapter 4—The European Pathway

1. Daniel 9:26.
2. Daniel 7:24.
3. Daniel 2:41,42.
4. Revelation 13:3.
5. Daniel 7:7,23; Revelation 13:7.
6. Ibid.
7. Daniel 7:24.
8. Ibid.

9. Ibid.
10. Daniel 7:25; 11:44,45; Revelation 13:7.
11. Daniel 7:25; Revelation 13:6.
12. Daniel 11:36; 2 Thessalonians 2:4; Revelation 13:8,12,15.
13. Daniel 11:38.
14. Daniel 11:39.
15. Daniel 7:25.
16. Daniel 7:25; Revelation 13:5.
17. Revelation 17:12.
18. Revelation 13:12.
19. Revelation 13:16,17.
20. Daniel 7:11-14,26,27.
21. *The Times Atlas of World History, Third Edition* (Hammond, Inc., 1989), p. 106.
22. *The New American Desk Encyclopedia* (Concord Reference Books, 1982).
23. Revelation 17:12-18.
24. Ralph Woodrow, *Babylon Mystery Religion* (Ralph Woodrow Evangelistic Association, 1966), pp. 13-15.
25. Michael Heseltine, *The Challenge of Europe, Can Britain Win?* (Weidenfeld and Nicolson, 1989), p. 9.
26. Daniel 2:43.
27. "Power Player: The awesome German giant," *U.S. News & World Report*, Apr. 1, 1991.
28. Nicholas Colchester and David Buchan, *Europe Relaunched: Truths and Illusions on the Way to 1992* (The Economist Books, 1990), p. 12.
29. Ibid, p. 8.
30. *New York Times,* Jan. 25, 1991.
31. Colchester and Buchan, *Europe*, pp. 160-61.
32. *The European*, Dec. 14-16, 1990.
33. "Uncalm Currencies," in *The Economist*, Feb. 16, 1991.
34. *The European*, Nov. 9-11, 1990.
35. *The Jewish Press*, Sep. 28, 1990.
36. *The Jerusalem Post International Edition*, Aug. 4, 1990.
37. *The European*, Mar. 1-3, 1991.
38. *The New York Times*, Apr. 18, 1991.
39. "Economy and Business Notes: North African Common Market," *World Press Review*, Sep. 1990.
40. *The New York Times*, Sep. 25, 1990.
41. Colchester and Buchan, *Europe*, pp. 180-81.
42. "Humanity at a Crossroads: The Holy See and the CSCE," in *Catholic International*, Mar. 1991.
43. "Libels in the Cathedral: Is the press guilty of anti-Catholic bias?" in *Newsweek*, Apr. 1, 1991.
44. "On Society: The gay tide of Catholic-bashing," in *U.S. News & World Report*, Apr. 1, 1991.

Chapter 5—The Russian Pathway

1. J.M. Roberts, *The Pelican History of the World*, (Penguin Books, 1987), p. 347.
2. Deanna Hodgin for *Insight* magazine, July 9, 1990.
3. *The Economist*, July 28, 1990.
4. Ibid.

5. *International Herald Tribune,* July 29, 1990.
6. *International Herald Tribune,* July 23, 1990.
7. *New York Times,* May 17, 1991.
8. *The European,* Nov. 30-Dec. 2, 1990.
9. *The European,* Mar. 15, 1990.
10. *Herald Statesman,* Oct. 8, 1990.
11. "Iran: A New Relationship," in *Newsweek,* Feb. 18, 1991.

Chapter 6—The Arab/Moslem Pathway
1. *Jewish Press,* Jan. 25, 1991.
2. Charles F. Pfeiffer, *Old Testament History* (Baker Book House, 1973), p. 473.
3. *New York Times,* Jan. 20, 1991.
4. Ezekiel 37:10.
5. *New York Times,* Mar. 22, 1991.
6. *The European,* Mar. 8-10, 1991.
7. Isaiah 14: 1,3.
8. *USA Today,* Feb. 8, 1991.
9. Joel 3:2
10. Rob Linsted, *The Next Move: Current Events in Bible Prophecy* (Bible Truth, 1985), p. 97.
11. *New York Times,* Jan. 19, 1991.
12. *New York Times,* Jan. 28, 1991.

Chapter 7—The Israeli Pathway
1. Genesis 25:5.
2. Genesis 25:18.
3. Genesis 17:21.
4. Josephus, translated by William Whiston, *The Works of Josephus Complete and Unabridged* (Hendrickson Publishers, 1987), p. 741.
5. Abba Eban, *Heritage:Civilization and the Jews* (Summit Books, 1984), pp. 87-88.
6. Ibid.
7. Ibid., p. 177.
8. Ibid., pp. 199-200.
9. *New York Times,* May 21, 1991.
10. Ronald Sanders, *The High Walls of Jerusalem: A History of the Balfour Declaration and the Birth of the British Mandate for Palestine* (Holt, Rinehart and Winston), p. 508.
11. Ibid., pp. 612-13.
12. Leviticus 25.
13. Zechariah 12:3.
14. *Jerusalem Post International Edition,* Apr. 13, 1991.
15. *Jewish Press,* June 29, 1990.
16. *Jewish Press* editorial, Mar. 22, 1991.
17. *Jewish Press,* June 29, 1990.
18. *Jewish Press* editorial, Mar. 22, 1991.
19. *New York Times* editorial, Mar. 19, 1991.
20. *Jewish Press* editorial, Mar. 22, 1991.
21. *Jewish Press,* June 29, 1990.
22. *Jerusalem Post International Edition,* Apr. 6, 1991.
23. *Jewish Press,* June 29, 1990.

24. *New York Times*, Apr. 19, 1991.
25. *Jerusalem Post International Edition*, Jan. 19, 1991.
26. *New York Times*, May 25, 1991.
27. *New York Times*, May 26, 1991.
28. Ibid.
29. Ibid.
30. *New York Times*, Mar. 15, 1991.
31. *New York Times*, Jan. 9, 1991.
32. *Jerusalem Post International Edition*, Jan. 12, 1991.
33. *New York Times*, Jan. 9, 1991.
34. "Time for a New Temple?" in *Time*, Oct. 16, 1989.
35. *Jewish Press*, Oct. 6, 1989.
36. In the same interview he indicated that he would not like to see the existing mosques on the Temple Mount—The Dome of the Rock and the Al Aqsa Mosque—destroyed, but would like them to be moved, perhaps to Mecca.
37. *Jerusalem Post International Edition*, Apr. 13, 1991.
38. "Where the Ancient Temple of Jerusalem Stood: Extant 'Foundation Stone' for the Ark of the Covenant is Identified," *Biblical Archaeology Review*, Mar./Apr. 1983.
39. *Jewish Press*, Nov. 3, 1989.
40. *Jerusalem Post International Edition*, Mar. 9, 1991.
41. *Jewish Press*, Oct. 13, 1989.
42. *Jerusalem Post International Edition*, Sep. 15, 1990.
43. *New York Times*, Feb. 16, 1989.
44. *Jewish Press*, Sep. 7, 1990.
45. *Jewish Press*, Aug. 3, 1990.
46. *Jerusalem Post International Edition*, May 4, 1991.
47. *Jewish Press*, Apr. 26, 1991.
48. *Jewish Press*, Feb. 8, 1991.
49. *Jewish Press*, Jan. 18, 1991.
50. *Jewish Press*, May 3, 1991.
51. Zechariah 12:2.
52. Zechariah 12:3.